FINANCING DISASTER RISK REDUCTION IN ASIA AND THE PACIFIC

A GUIDE FOR POLICY MAKERS

DECEMBER 2020

ADB

Contents

Figures and Boxes

Acknowledgments

This guide was prepared under the technical assistance project Integrated Disaster Risk Management Fund: Sharing Lessons, Achievements, and Best Practice of the Asian Development Bank (ADB) financed by the Government of Canada through the ADB-administered Integrated Disaster Risk Management Fund.

The guide was prepared under the overall supervision of Steven Goldfinch, disaster risk management specialist, Sustainable Development and Climate Change Department (SDCC), ADB. Grendel J. Saldevar Perez, senior operations assistant, SDCC, and Anna Karmina Ong-Pantig (consultant) provided invaluable overall coordination support in finalizing the document.

Renard Teipelke (principal consultant, AECOM) led the development of the guide, with Antje Lang, Cerin Kizhakkethottam, and Elliot Aguirre from AECOM providing valuable inputs to the internal discussion and review of different versions of the note. Claudette Rodrigo and Edith Creus did the infographics and layout.

The document benefited significantly from discussions with and comments from Charlotte Benson, principal disaster risk management specialist; Thomas Kessler, principal finance specialist (disaster insurance), and Frederic Asseline, principal climate change specialist (climate finance), SDCC, ADB; and Sarah Wade-Apicella, programme management officer, UN Office for Disaster Risk Reduction (UNDRR).

Abbreviations

ADB	Asian Development Bank
ADF	Asian Development Fund (of ADB)
ASEAN	Association of Southeast Asian Nations
COP	(United Nations Climate Change) Conference of the Parties
DRM	disaster risk management
DRR	disaster risk reduction
EIB	Environmental Impact Bond
GCF	Green Climate Fund
GDP	gross domestic product
NDA	National Designated Authorities (GCF)
PPP	public–private partnership
SDG	Sustainable Development Goal
UNDRR	United Nations Office for Disaster Risk Reduction
UNFCCC	United Nations Framework Convention on Climate Change

Executive Summary

To strengthen resilience, disaster risk reduction seeks to (i) prevent new disaster risk, (ii) reduce existing disaster risk, and (iii) manage residual risk. The business case for resilience investments is compelling with an average $1 spent saving $4–$7 in response. Disaster risk reduction is especially relevant in Asia and the Pacific, because it is anticipated that the growth in average estimated annual disaster losses will outpace gross domestic product (GDP) growth in the region. However, the majority of funding has been focused on post-disaster recovery and reconstruction rather than disaster risk reduction.

This publication is intended to guide policy makers and administrators in developing member countries and stakeholders interested in financing disaster risk reduction. It seeks to support countries in addressing the financial underinvestment in disaster risk reduction by (i) setting the scene and confirming the business case for advancing disaster risk reduction finance; (ii) outlining the context of disaster risk reduction and its finance; (iii) conceptualizing approaches, types, and instrument prioritization criteria for disaster risk reduction finance; (iv) explaining instruments and mechanisms that can accelerate the speed and increase the scale of disaster risk reduction finance by the public and private sectors, as well as international development organizations; and (v) outlining key steps for governments to further advance disaster risk reduction finance.

There are many ways to support the institutionalization of disaster risk reduction across the areas of risk assessments and understanding, planning and decision-making, as well as acting upon and implementing plans and projects. Improvements in inter-governmental relations, adequate fiscal management, and reforms to the regulatory system are key enabling factors to disaster risk reduction finance in the public sector.

Since government funding alone is not sufficient in scale to meet the financing needs for disaster risk reduction, private sector participation has to expand. For that, the contextual setting needs to be more inviting for private sector investments, finance instruments will have to further mature, and the business model of disaster risk reduction projects needs to be operationally and financially scalable. On the one hand, the supply side of private finance instruments and funding will have to further tailor its strategic offering for corresponding disaster risk reduction investments. On the other hand, the demand side (typically public sector) will need to increase its capacity in terms of financial literacy, familiarity, and willingness to engage with other actors.

It is important to also recognize the strategic position of bilateral and multilateral development banks and United Nations (UN) agencies in supporting disaster risk reduction finance, as they (i) convene and intermediate between different public and private actors nationally and globally; (ii) offer a variety of financial, policy, technical, and capacity development products and services to support an enabling environment for investment; (iii) have developed extensive experience with different structural and nonstructural interventions; and (iv) hold large and comparatively affordable resources.

Common approaches to disaster risk reduction finance include: (i) implementing stand-alone investment projects, (ii) devising dedicated funds for disaster risk reduction measures that different departments and government entities can draw from, and (iii) funding disaster risk reduction as a budget line within sector department budgets. The types of disaster risk reduction finance can be differentiated into recurrent (operational) expenditures and capital (investment) expenditures, whereby nonstructural measures should receive equal attention to structural (physical) measures. This publication provides assessment criteria to help screen the landscape of available instruments and better understand where each one's advantages and risks lie. Due to the varied and often interlinking nature of project risks, the presented instruments often need to be jointly deployed in the implementation of different structural and nonstructural measures.

Broadly categorized into own-source revenues, grants and transfers, debt, and equity, instruments for disaster risk reduction finance are presented alongside practical examples from Asia and the Pacific, as well as globally. In terms of own-source revenues, governments have a range of instruments through taxes, tariffs, fees, and fines, while land-value capture and other nonfinancial tools provide avenues to indirectly advance disaster risk reduction.

Grant and transfer instruments are dominated by earmarked, top-up (incremental), performance-based or conditional grants, as well as competitive grant funds. In addition, cost-sharing programs are an effective mechanism for disaster risk reduction finance, as they require co-financing and corresponding ownership and commitment from receiving entities.

Among the debt instruments, loans play a crucial role, with disaster risk reduction projects being funded by both concessional and commercial loans and loan facilities and/or funds, or at least supported through incentivized (discounted) lending rates. Growing in importance and scale, the bond market has evolved and is adapting to the needs of resilience-focused investments with instruments such as green, resilience, environmental impact, and Sustainable Development Goal (SDG) bonds.

With regard to equity instruments, a wide variety of instruments caters to the varying investment horizons and risk profiles of different investors. Public–private partnerships have shown potential in integrating disaster risk reduction into infrastructure facilities, while viability gap funding mechanisms are being deployed to emerging resilience technologies. Instruments around co-investment funds, blended finance, aggregation, and securitization do furthermore expand capital market participation in resilience investments.

International development finance for disaster risk reduction offers additional support through global funds, trust funds, specialist mechanisms and programs, disaster risk financing and insurance, as well as programmatic support from early technical assistance through to disaster risk reduction loans. In that way, international development organizations support with strategic partnerships, finance, and knowledge.

This publication provides case studies that illustrate how some countries have been moving ahead in prioritizing disaster risk reduction and resilience-building in their development and related investments. More can and must be done. Therefore, this publication provides guidance—including top tips across the five chapters—for developing member countries and interested stakeholders to scale-up disaster risk reduction finance in light of current and future climate and disaster risks.

KEY MESSAGES

> "Every 100 years, the Association of Southeast Asian Nations region on average will face disaster losses totaling **$18 billion** or 1% of regional gross domestic product.

Source: World Bank. 2012. ASEAN – Advancing Disaster Risk Financing and Insurance in ASEAN Member States: Framework and Options for Implementation. Volume 1: Main Report. Washington, DC.

> "If the **1.5 degrees Celsius** threshold is breached, the possibilities to adapt to climate change will diminish as ecosystem services collapse."

Source: UNDRR. 2019. Global Assessment Report on Disaster Risk Reduction. Geneva.

> "The long-term rate of growth in disaster losses in the Asia and Pacific region is presently outpacing growth in GDP, making the need for **strengthened resilience** ever more urgent."

Source: ADB. 2013. Investing in Resilience. Ensuring a Disaster-Resistant Future. Manila.

> "**Disasters** have a particularly detrimental impact on the poorest members of society, widening income and gender disparities and affecting nutritional, health, and educational status of this group disproportionally."

Source: ADB. 2017. Disaster Risk Management and Country Partnership Strategies. A Practical Guide. Manila.

> "We must **act** with **urgency** and with greater ambition, proportional to the scale of threat."

Source: UNDRR. 2019. Global Assessment Report on Disaster Risk Reduction. Geneva. p. xi.

> "**Not investing** in disaster risk management is a **missed opportunity** for social, economic, and environmental progress."

Source: ODI and World Bank. 2015. Unlocking the 'Triple Dividend' of Resilience. Why Investing in Disaster Risk Management Pays Off. London and Washington, DC.

"Risks from **climate change** are uncertain, but in some cases, they are now **foreseeable** based on available scientific evidence."

Source: OECD. 2018. Climate-Resilient Infrastructure. Policy Perspectives. OECD Environment Policy Paper No. 14. Paris.

"Disaster risk reduction is about **safeguarding** achieved development."

Source: UNDRR. 2015. Disaster Risk Reduction Private Sector Partnership. Geneva.

"Appropriate **investments** into adaptation and resilience can work within the uncertainties of climate change and disaster risks and result in **multiple benefits** to society."

Source: UNDRR (UNISDR). 2019. Global Assessment Report on Disaster Risk Reduction. Geneva.

"Disaster risk **reduction** requires an all-of-society engagement and partnership."

Source: United Nations. 2015. Sendai Framework for Disaster Risk Reduction 2015–2030. New York.

"Tackling climate change, **building climate** and **disaster resilience**, and enhancing environmental sustainability are interconnected agendas and are central to the achievement of the Sustainable Development Goals."

Source: ADB. 2019. Strategy 2030 Operational Plan for Priority 3: Tackling Climate Change, Building Climate and Disaster Resilience, and Enhancing Environmental Sustainability, 2019–2024. Manila.

"There is a need for **focused action** within and across sectors at local, national, regional, and global levels in four priority areas, including Priority 3: Investing in disaster risk reduction for resilience."

Source: United Nations. 2015. Sendai Framework for Disaster Risk Reduction 2015–2030. New York.

1 Introduction

Setting the Scene

When it comes to disaster events, Asia and the Pacific suffers more than half of all people affected and a staggering 70% of the deaths and missing people worldwide.[1] It also experienced the largest economic losses at 43% of the global total between 2005 and 2017, which was more than its global share in gross domestic product (GDP). While the region's higher-income countries have the largest absolute economic impacts from disasters, it is low- and middle-income countries that have to deal with higher relative levels of risks and large economic impacts on their comparatively small GDPs.[2]

Statistics indicate a growth in estimated annual losses from disasters that is outpacing GDP growth in Asia and the Pacific—meaning that disaster losses are a serious threat to the development goals of the region.[3] This includes immediate direct losses from disasters, but also, for instance, indirect losses on supply chains, wider impacts on the tourism sector, and macroeconomic repercussions on fiscal stability. Indeed, developing economies in Asia and the Pacific will need to invest around $1.7 trillion each year between 2016 and 2030 to sustain their economic growth, eradicate remaining poverty, and respond to climate mitigation and adaptation needs.[4] Urgent action is, therefore, required in reducing disaster risks through comprehensive, cross-sector strategies and investments.

> **TOP TIP**
>
> Proactive measures to reduce disaster risks are required as climate change will aggravate existing risks, with impacts outpacing economic growth in Asia and the Pacific.

The most recent international agendas recognize the importance of disaster risk reduction toward this end (Appendix 1). In particular, the Sendai Framework (2015) encourages public and private sector actors, as well as civil society to avoid decisions that would create (additional) risk, develop risk-reducing actions, and support communities and systems (e.g., infrastructure networks and financial markets) to build resilience. Related international agendas, such as the Paris Agreement (2016) and the Agenda 2030/Sustainable Development Goals (SDGs) (2015) also underscore the interlinkage of disaster risk reduction and climate change adaptation, and highlight opportunities to building resilience into sustainable development.[5]

---

[1]   ADB. 2011. Asia 2050: Realizing the Asian Century; UNDRR. 2019. Global Assessment Report on Disaster Risk Reduction. Geneva.
[2]   ADB. 2017. *Disaster Risk Management and Country Partnership Strategies. A Practical Guide.* Manila
[3]   ADB. 2013. *Investing in Resilience. Ensuring a Disaster-Resistant Future.* Manila.
[4]   ADB. 2017. *Meeting Asia's Infrastructure Needs.* Manila.
[5]   ADB. 2019. *Strategy 2030 Operational Plan for Priority 3: Tackling Climate Change, Building Climate and Disaster Resilience, and Enhancing Environmental Sustainability, 2019–2024.* Manila.

As illustrated in Figure 1.1, disaster risk reduction advocates for prevention (to avoid disasters), mitigation (to minimize disaster impacts), and better preparedness (anticipation before disasters strike). It incorporates both structural (physical) and nonstructural (planning and management) measures, which can save lives, reduce the impacts from disasters, and allow for more effective development and reconstruction.[6]

Figure 1.1: Objectives and Measures of Disaster Risk Reduction

Understanding Risk

Hazard Frequency and Intensity × Exposure   Vulnerability

Disaster Risk Reduction

Prevention   Mitigation   Preparedness

Structural Measures   Non-Structural Measures

Source: Author.

Disaster risk reduction also requires close consideration of current and projected climate change impacts and their influence on the exposure and vulnerability of people and assets. Future climate and disaster risks do not simply follow linear trajectories based on historical patterns. Therefore, policy development, infrastructure planning, and prioritization have to incorporate the best available data and methods for decision-making under conditions of uncertainty to future-proof assets.[7]

Business Case for Disaster Risk Reduction

Many investment decisions come with disaster and climate risks. If misinformed, development actions can exacerbate existing risks and have detrimental impacts on "neighboring" elements in their network or region (footnote 3). For example, investing in coastal assets may promote economic development and tourism in the

---

6   UN Inter-Agency Task Force on Financing for Development. 2019. *Climate Finance, Disaster Risk and Environmental Resilience*. Website. https://developmentfinance.un.org/climate-finance-disaster-risk-and-environmental-resilience.

7   OECD. 2018. Climate-Resilient Infrastructure. *Policy Perspectives. OECD Environment Policy Paper No. 14. Paris; Climate Bonds Initiative. 2019. Climate Resilience Principles. A Framework for Assessing Climate Resilience Investments*. London.

short term, but may increase risk in the long term as these assets contend with sea-level rise, or the development itself may increase coastal erosion and associated flood risk.

With climate change projections indicating higher average temperatures and a greater frequency in extreme weather events in the region,[8] service disruptions with cascading effects are increasingly likely, and certain assets are at risk of becoming "stranded"— i.e., an asset which once had value is either losing it or no longer has value— in this case, due to the impacts of or technological changes occurring due to climate and disaster risk.[9] This, in turn, can have significant impacts at the individual, household, and firm level in terms of lost money, time, and well-being, while also resulting in economic welfare losses and political instability (with climate and disaster-induced mass migration as a scenario already now emerging across the world).[10]

To be sure, reducing disaster risk and taking risk-informed decisions is a feasible and cost-effective way to future-proof new development and retrofit existing infrastructure to withstand current and emerging climate and disaster risks.[11] Resilient infrastructure offers what has been coined a "triple dividend" (Figure 1.2).[12] The business case for resilience investments is compelling with an average $1 spent saving $4–$7 in response.[13] Cost–benefit analyses specifically conducted for the Asia and Pacific region have shown ratios from 1:2 to as high as 1:55 in terms of the benefits from investing in disaster-resilient measures (footnote 3).

However, significant barriers remain to financing disaster risk reduction (and related climate adaptation measures), as financing has yet to match the scale of existing (and future) disaster risks.[14] Both public and private actors are underinvesting in disaster risk reduction. Instead, funds and budgets are often overly focused on disaster response and recovery, with only a fraction dedicated to preventing disasters in the first place.[15]

Figure 1.2: Triple Dividend of Resilient Infrastructure Investments

1st Dividend: Avoided losses from disasters

2nd Dividend: Development through investments by households and businesses

3rd Dividend: Positive economic, social, and environmental co-benefits

Source: Author.

8   IPCC. 2014. Asia. In: Climate Change 2014: Impacts, Adaptation, and Vulnerability. Part B: Regional Aspects. Contribution of Working Group II to the Fifth Assessment Report of the Intergovernmental Panel on Climate Change. New York.
9   Chan, C. and N. Amerasinghe. 2018. Deploying Adaptation Finance for Maximum Impact. Commentary. Washington DC: World Resources Institute; Caldecott, B.. 2018. *Stranded Assets and the Environment*. Abingdon: Routledge.
10   World Bank. 2019. *Lifelines: The Resilient Infrastructure Opportunity*. Washington, DC.
11   Jackson, D. 2011. *Effective Financial Mechanisms at the National and Local Level for Disaster Risk Reduction. Paper Written for the Mid Term Review of the UNISDR Hyogo Framework for Action*. New York: United Nations Capital Development Fund.
12   ODI and World Bank. 2015. Unlocking the 'Triple Dividend' of Resilience. Why Investing in Disaster Risk Management Pays Off. London and Washington, DC.
13   UNDRR. 2015. *Disaster Risk Reduction Private Sector Partnership*. Geneva.
14   Resch, E. et al. 2018. Mainstreaming, Accessing and Institutionalising Finance for Climate Change Adaptation. *Action on Climate Today Learning Paper*. Oxford: Oxford Policy Management.
15   Micale, V., B. Tonkonogy, and F. Mazza. 2018. *Understanding and Increasing Finance for Climate Adaptation in Developing Countries*. San Francisco: Climate Policy Initiative and Adelphi.

TOP TIP

Revisit budget allocations and actual spending on disaster risk management. Money spent on reducing disaster risk can save multiple times the costs that disaster impacts cause.

To illustrate the gap in financing, international aid from 1991 to 2010 had a resource envelope of some $3.03 trillion, of which around $106.7 billion went to disasters, and only $13.5 billion of that ended up in disaster risk reduction funding—barely 13% (0.4% of the total).[16] Moreover, from 2005 to 2017, $137 billion was provided in development assistance for disasters, with $9.60 out of every $10 spent on emergency response, reconstruction, relief, and rehabilitation; while less than 4%, $5.2 billion, was invested into disaster prevention and preparedness.[17]

This publication speaks to this discrepancy in financing disaster risk reduction by (i) providing an overview of the opportunities for advancing disaster risk reduction and its financing (Chapter 1), (ii) explaining key concepts of financing disaster risk reduction (Chapter 2), (iii) collating instruments and mechanisms that can accelerate the speed and increase the scale of financing future-proof development investments (Chapter 3), and (iv) outlining steps for governments to advance disaster risk reduction finance (Chapter 4). Top tips throughout the four chapters offer guidance on how to apply the knowledge on disaster risk reduction finance in practice. The appendixes provide more detailed elaboration on specific policies, case studies, and instruments.

---

16   Kellet, J. and A. Caravani. 2013. *Financing Disaster Risk Reduction. A 20 Year Story of International Aid.* London: ODI and GFDRR.
17   UNDRR. 2019. *Global Assessment Report on Disaster Risk Reduction.* Geneva.

2 The Context of Disaster Risk Reduction and Finance

Elements for Institutionalizing Disaster Risk Reduction

There is a wide range of good practice examples for reducing disaster risk and a plethora of tools and guidance notes available to inform the development and planning of resilient infrastructure investments.[18] However, pragmatic measures and quick fixes will not suffice in addressing climate and disaster risks that are deeply embedded in infrastructure networks, economic markets, and governance systems and processes. Most national and, particularly, subnational governments are highly exposed and vulnerable to a range of hazards and impacts stemming from a lack of catalytic investments in disaster risk reduction, combined with a shortfall in long-term strategic approaches and institutional reforms.[19]

Figure 2.1 provides a structured illustration on key elements that can support more institutionalized disaster risk reduction in the public sector (footnote 3). Furthermore, Appendix 2 summarizes five entry points identified by the Global Assessment Report by the United Nations Office for Disaster Risk Reduction (UNDRR) on how to advance resilience against disaster risks more broadly (footnote 17).

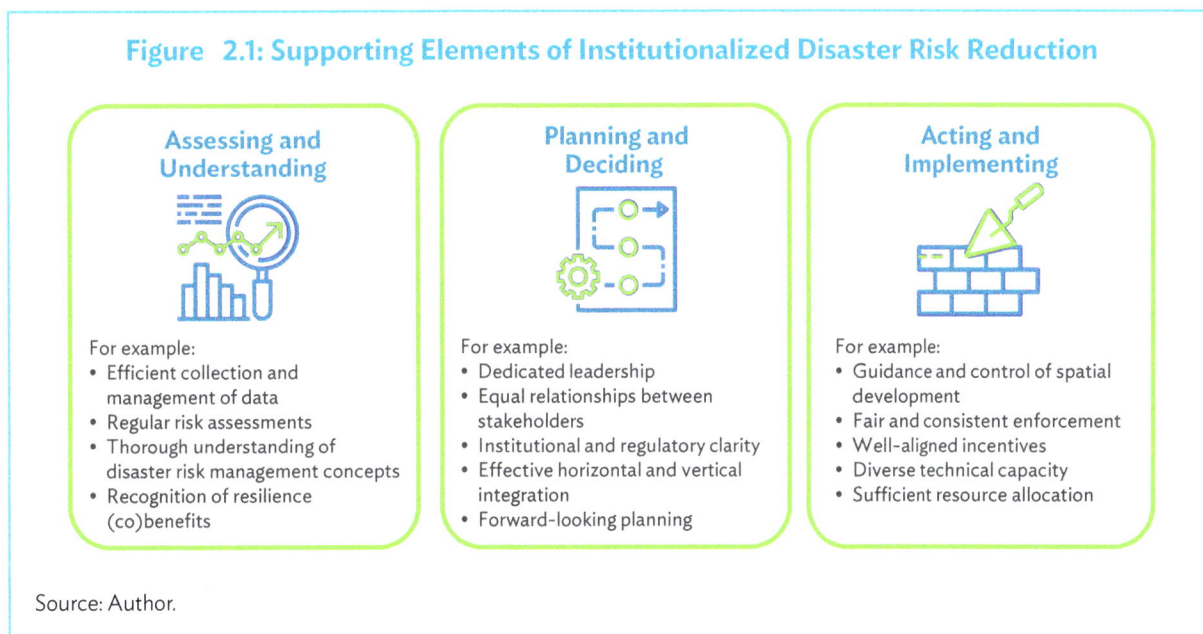

Figure 2.1: Supporting Elements of Institutionalized Disaster Risk Reduction

Assessing and Understanding

For example:
- Efficient collection and management of data
- Regular risk assessments
- Thorough understanding of disaster risk management concepts
- Recognition of resilience (co)benefits

Planning and Deciding

For example:
- Dedicated leadership
- Equal relationships between stakeholders
- Institutional and regulatory clarity
- Effective horizontal and vertical integration
- Forward-looking planning

Acting and Implementing

For example:
- Guidance and control of spatial development
- Fair and consistent enforcement
- Well-aligned incentives
- Diverse technical capacity
- Sufficient resource allocation

Source: Author.

---

18 European Commission. 2018. *Climate Change Adaptation of Major Infrastructure Projects. A Stock-Taking of Available Resources to Assist the Development of Climate Resilient Infrastructure.* Brussels.
19 Wilkinson, E. et al. 2017. *Delivering Disaster Risk Reduction by 2030. Pathways to Progress.* London: ODI.

Assessing and understanding. Knowing the risks to which a neighborhood, infrastructure utility, or economic sector is exposed to is the first step to inform disaster risk reduction. This includes assessing the exposure of people and assets to those hazards, and the vulnerability that communities or infrastructure networks may have that could further increase or mitigate their susceptibility to disaster risk impacts. Improving data availability, accessibility, and quality has become a key priority for organizations and institutions seeking to address disaster risk.[20] Many initiatives around traditional and alternative data collection and processing (e.g., using remote sensing or community mapping) have been piloted and scaled-up over recent years.[21] Building on this improved understanding of risk, it is crucial to clearly make the case for the benefits of risk assessments and improved knowledge as it can provide a valuable impetus to influence political priority-setting.

TOP TIP

Make disaster and climate risk assessment findings and data available to the public, private, and civil society sectors. Better information can improve people's decision-making.

Planning and deciding. Vulnerable groups disproportionately experience the greatest impacts from disasters—however, they often lack a political voice to make their concerns and suggestions heard (footnote 17). Short-term thinking, driven by political election cycles and a greater focus on economic growth, can prevent a more strategic approach to disaster risk reduction. As a result, disasters trigger higher losses which, in turn, uphold existing political attention on post-disaster response, recovery, and partly reconstruction.[22] Additionally, disaster risk reduction and management plans that are not up-to-date or sufficiently robust can leave institutional and regulatory ambiguity following a disaster in terms of responsible agencies and pre-disaster allocated relief and recovery funding readily available and accessible for disbursement.[23] It is, therefore, crucial to mainstream systematic disaster risk reduction into regulatory frameworks, institutions, budgetary processes (e.g. through budget tagging), as well as investment design and prioritization. This can help create a system with proactive planning and budgeting from disaster risk reduction through to timely disaster response, recovery, and reconstruction.

It can be challenging to address disaster risk reduction due to its cross-sector nature. This is even truer when taking climate change adaptation into account, where often different line ministries (e.g., finance, civil protection, environment, and public works) are responsible for different elements that jointly influence risk reduction and resilience-building measures (footnote 12). Effective mainstreaming of disaster risk reduction benefits from two interlinked features: (i) proper horizontal coordination based on a defined legal framework, and (ii) clear vertical coordination between national-level agencies and subnational governments about assigned responsibilities, authority, and budget allocations. The example of the Philippines illustrates that even in a complex legal and regulatory setting, disaster risk reduction can be advanced in institutional and budgetary terms (Box 2.1).[24]

Acting and implementing. Scaling-up disaster risk reduction efforts requires putting into practice related laws, policies, and programs. Particularly in dynamic and growing economies such as in Asia, disaster risk reduction—similar to other long-term oriented policy areas—benefits from smart spatial development guidance and control instead of haphazard growth.[25] It also entails the enforcement of updated civil protection legislation or new standards in the infrastructure and building sectors to accommodate higher climate and disaster resilience (footnote 17). Well-trained government staff, as well as experts in various sectors (e.g., utilities and building

[20] UNDRR. 2017. *Disaster-Related Data for Sustainable Development – Sendai Framework Data Readiness Review 2017, Global Summary Report.* Geneva.
[21] World Bank. 2014. *Understanding Risk in an Evolving World. Emerging Best Practices in Natural Disaster Risk Assessment.* Washington, DC.
[22] Kellet, J., A. Caravani, and F. Pichon. 2014. *Financing Disaster Risk Reduction: Towards a Coherent and Comprehensive Approach.* London: ODI.
[23] World Bank. 2013. *Financing Post-Disaster Recovery and Reconstruction Operations: Developing an Institutional Mechanism to Ensure the Effective Use of Financial Resources.* Washington, DC.
[24] Villacin, D. T. 2017. *A Review of Philippine Government Disaster Financing for Recovery and Reconstruction.* Discussion Paper Series No. 2017-21. Manila: Philippine Institute for Development Studies.
[25] UNDRR. 2019. *Disaster Risk Reduction in the Philippines. Status Report 2019.* Bangkok.

Box 2.1: Philippines' National Disaster Risk Reduction and Management Framework

The National Disaster Risk Reduction and Management Framework (NDRRMF), established in 2011, lays out the Philippines' disaster risk management priorities and institutional arrangements. It supports mainstreaming disaster risk reduction priorities into development planning via a framework outlined by the National Economic and Development Authority. The NDRRMF has stand-alone funding, supplemented by the Local Disaster Risk Reduction and Management Funds (LDRRMF).

Provincial, city, and municipal levels contribute to the NDRRMF through local disaster risk reduction management plans and a minimum of 5% of local government income is earmarked for their LDRRMFs. Of this, 70% is reserved specifically for the mitigation fund for use against disaster prevention, mitigation, preparedness, response, rehabilitation, and recovery projects as identified in a city's local disaster risk reduction and management plan and as integrated in its annual investment program.

However, the NDRRMF faces several challenges. For one, the mechanism for disbursement for pre-disaster funding is less clear than for recovery funding. Additionally, the annual allocation reverts back to the General Fund if it is not used within 2 years. Uncertainty remains about the level of funding for NDRRMF, which would be eliminated if legal provisions existed to enforce a predetermined amount of budget allocated to the fund as exists, for instance, with Mexico's Natural Disaster Prevention Fund or FOPREDEN (Appendix 4).

Sources: ADB. 2016. *Incentives for Reducing Disaster Risk in Urban Areas. Experiences from Da Nang (Viet Nam), Kathmandu Valley (Nepal), and Naga City (Philippines)*. Manila.
ADB. 2018. *Philippine City Disaster Insurance Pool. Rationale and Design*. Manila.
UNDRR (UNISDR). 2019. *Disaster Risk Reduction in the Philippines. Status Report 2019*. Bangkok. p. 16–17.
Villacin, D. T. 2017. *A Review of Philippine Government Disaster Financing for Recovery and Reconstruction*. Discussion Paper Series No. 2017-21. Manila: Philippine Institute for Development Studies.

construction professions), are important to understand natural hazards, exposure, and vulnerability, and to devise feasible solutions to address climate and disaster risks. In addition to capacities, sufficient financial resources are required for realizing disaster risk reduction projects across sectors (footnote 22).

Enabling Factors for Public Sector Disaster Risk Reduction Finance

Several factors can be identified that can enable the financing aspects around disaster risk reduction in the public sector (Figure 2.2) (footnote 17).

Inter-governmental relations. Due to the cross-sector nature of disaster risks and their management, the often-complex public finance regimes in many countries do not facilitate an easy flow of funding into disaster risk reduction measures. On the other hand, governments with good transparency and accountability in their spending often enjoy advantages in tracking, evaluating, and potentially redirecting funding for different disaster risk reduction measures. This also requires clearly defined roles and responsibilities of different national and subnational entities in terms of reducing, managing, and responding to disaster risks (footnote 24). Furthermore, well-designed incentives can promote cross-sector programs jointly coordinated and implemented by different agencies.

Fiscal management. Recognizing the full risk exposure of communities and assets, funding to disaster risk reduction needs to be significantly larger than it currently is (footnote 22). Besides the envelope of funding, fund flows and budgetary processes are crucial for how efficiently money arrives in the corresponding projects on the

Figure 2.2: Enabling Factors for Public Sector Disaster Risk Reduction Finance

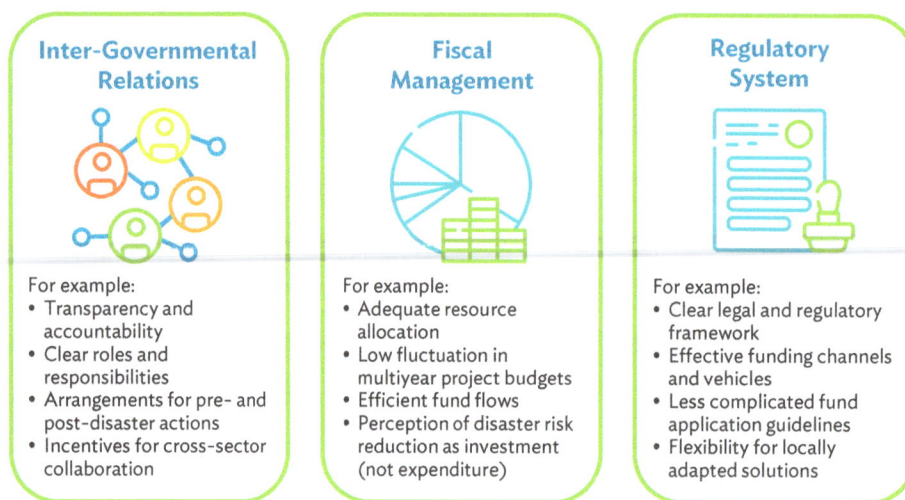

Inter-Governmental Relations

For example:
- Transparency and accountability
- Clear roles and responsibilities
- Arrangements for pre- and post-disaster actions
- Incentives for cross-sector collaboration

Fiscal Management

For example:
- Adequate resource allocation
- Low fluctuation in multiyear project budgets
- Efficient fund flows
- Perception of disaster risk reduction as investment (not expenditure)

Regulatory System

For example:
- Clear legal and regulatory framework
- Effective funding channels and vehicles
- Less complicated fund application guidelines
- Flexibility for locally adapted solutions

Source: Author.

> **TOP TIP**
>
> Systemic changes to reducing and managing disaster risks take time. Allocate and secure multiyear budgets for related programs and projects.

ground. Given their multisector and typically multiyear nature, disaster risk reduction programs and projects can be detrimentally impacted where funding fluctuates or where it does not provide for both structural and nonstructural measures to incrementally strengthen the resilience of people and assets (footnote 3). Reframing these resilience measures as a capital investment with a "triple dividend," as opposed to an additional expenditure, provides an opportunity to increase disaster risk reduction funding in the public sector.

Regulatory system. The use of different instruments in financing disaster risk reduction requires a corresponding regulatory framework that authorizes national or subnational entities to utilize certain instruments or financing mechanisms, such as issuing bonds or taking out international development loans. It is also important to tailor application and disbursement systems for disaster risk reduction funds in a way that allows agencies—including those with less capacity and experience—to effectively receive financial support (also see Appendix 4). While proven resilience interventions can be recommended for application across different locations, the regulatory framework of disaster risk reduction initiatives should avoid one-sided or "cookie-cutter"-type interventions and invite locally adapted solutions (footnote 22).

Matching Public and Private Actors in Financing Disaster Risk Reduction

Public sector funding—even where supported by international development assistance—will not be sufficient in scale to meet the financing needs for disaster risk reduction without private sector

> **TOP TIP**
>
> Convening public and private stakeholders can help to exchange views on how to improve existing systems for different actors to contribute to disaster risk reduction finance.

participation (footnote 17). Recognizing the increasing engagement of private actors in disaster risk management (Box 2.2), there are several factors that characterize the "financing ecosystem" where public and private actors can be better matched for increased financing of disaster risk reduction (Figure 2.3) (footnote 15).

Box 2.2: Private Sector Engagement in Disaster Risk Management

Increasingly, the private sector has become more systematic in response to a heightened awareness for how climate and disaster risks do not only endanger communities, but also businesses and markets within them. This entails a move beyond more classic corporate social responsibility (CSR) activities to companies supporting (local) disaster risk reduction measures either through their own outreach schemes or through dedicated community organizations. Among developing countries in Asia and the Pacific, the Philippines is an example of a country with advanced private sector engagement in disaster risk management.

For instance, the Philippine Business for Social Progress, a business-led nongovernment organization, has a dedicated disaster risk reduction and management relief assistance under its environment program providing financial support to victims of calamities and facilitating rehabilitation and response initiatives after a disaster event. The Philippine Disaster Recovery Foundation, on the other hand, launched the first national private sector Emergency Operations Center coordinating and building capacity in disaster prevention, mitigation, preparedness, response, recovery, and rehabilitation activities. It also has a dedicated knowledge and learning resource center (Prelab) promoting the disciplines of resilience-building business continuity management, disaster risk reduction, and climate change adaptation.

Sources: Kellet, J., A. Caravani, and F. Pichon. 2014. *Financing Disaster Risk Reduction: Towards a Coherent and Comprehensive Approach*. London: ODI.
PBSP disaster risk reduction and management website. https://www.pbsp.org.ph/?page_id=10495.
Further information on: PDRF. 2020. Emergency Operation Center. https://www.pdrf.org/eoc/functions/.

Figure 2.3: Matching Public and Private Actors in Financing Disaster Risk Reduction

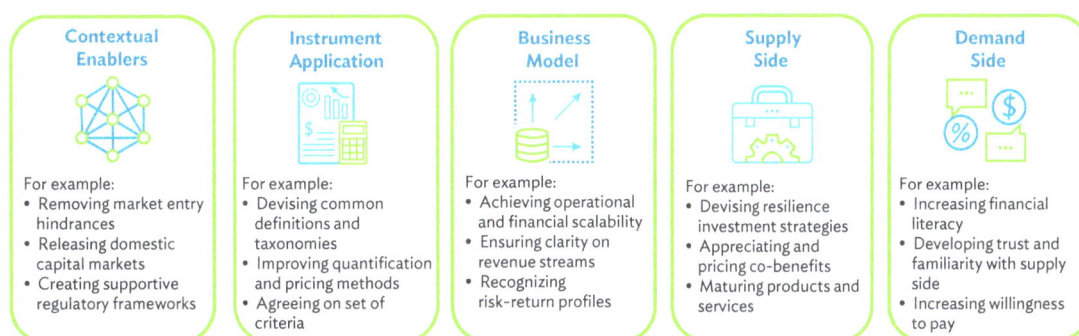

Contextual Enablers	Instrument Application	Business Model	Supply Side	Demand Side
For example: • Removing market entry hindrances • Releasing domestic capital markets • Creating supportive regulatory frameworks	For example: • Devising common definitions and taxonomies • Improving quantification and pricing methods • Agreeing on set of criteria	For example: • Achieving operational and financial scalability • Ensuring clarity on revenue streams • Recognizing risk-return profiles	For example: • Devising resilience investment strategies • Appreciating and pricing co-benefits • Maturing products and services	For example: • Increasing financial literacy • Developing trust and familiarity with supply side • Increasing willingness to pay

Source: Author.

Contextual enablers. The piloting and the scaling up of new or adapted instruments for disaster risk reduction financing benefit from supportive regulatory frameworks (see for instance Box 4.4 and Box 7.3). This can include the removal of market-entry barriers to allow global investors and instrument providers to access domestic markets or releasing domestic savings for different investments into disaster risk reduction.[26]

---

[26]   Suminski, S., A. Panda, and P. J. Lambert. 2019. Disaster Insurance in Developing Asia: An Analysis of Market-Based Schemes. *ADB Economics Working Paper Series No. 590*. Manila: ADB.

Instrument application. Assessing disaster risks and applying the findings to the design of structural and nonstructural resilience measures is complex. Likewise, the pricing of such risks and the development and tailoring of instruments to finance such measures can be difficult and costly. Recently, common definitions and understandings of resilience have been evolving, whereby clearer taxonomies are emerging for what constitutes resilient infrastructure from an investment perspective.[27] While there are evolving methodologies to quantify the performance and benefits of disaster risk reduction investments, accessing the requisite information to develop a robust assessment and monitoring performance over a project's lifetime are still challenging, particularly in data-scarce contexts (footnote 7).

TOP TIP

Private sector finance is profit-oriented. It is key to understand investors' perspective, appetite for risk, and their value-add in disaster risk reduction projects without losing sight of sustainable development objectives.

Business model. Investments into climate change adaptation and disaster risk reduction in many sectors have been struggling in terms of income streams, which are often easier to identify in climate change mitigation projects (e.g., solar farms) or more traditional private sector investments (e.g., toll roads). Nevertheless, while the up-front technology costs of some disaster resilience investments can be higher and their operation may require additional skills and dedicated resources, corresponding interventions have been changing from small pilot projects to larger-scale schemes.[28] This change in size and scalability improves the attractiveness of these investments in terms of their risk-return profiles (footnote 27). Examples are emerging across different countries and sectors globally, including bond issuances for fluvial flood prevention schemes (Germany), sustainability targets-linked loans in the agricultural production sector (People's Republic of China), green infrastructure-financing stormwater retention credits (United States), rehabilitation-focused equity investments in the agroforestry sector (Brazil), and sustainable marine resources-focused blue bond issuance for the tourism and fisheries sectors (Seychelles) (also see Appendix 7).[29]

Supply side. Many investors have historically lacked a comprehensive strategy and product offering to invest in the growing adaptation and resilience sector, although recent years have seen a positive shift in terms of investor focus toward green and climate-friendly investments.[30] This is linked to improved knowledge and increasing disclosure of portfolio risks, as well as a more refined recognition of investment co-benefits (footnote 27). Based on early experiences, products and services for disaster and climate resilience are maturing.

Demand side. Financial literacy in the public sector has been limited in terms of understanding the different private finance instruments, their requirements, and fiscal and regulatory implications. Slowly, trust and familiarity are developing with investors, their products and services, as well as the technical language. This is important, as reliance on traditional (public) funding channels is insufficient to meet the resourcing needs toward disaster risk reduction (footnote 26). Where risks are properly assessed and benefits of disaster risk reduction investments are evaluated, the willingness to pay for related services and the readiness to engage with other (private) actors can put national and subnational governments at the forefront of innovative disaster risk reduction finance (also see Appendix 7).

---

[27] Climate Bonds Initiative. 2019. *Climate Resilience Principles. A Framework for Assessing Climate Resilience Investments*. London.
[28] Wouter Botzen W. J. et al. 2019. Integrated Disaster Risk Management and Adaptation. In Mechler R.et al., eds. *Loss and Damage from Climate Change. Climate Risk Management, Policy and Governance*. Springer, Cham. https://doi.org/10.1007/978-3-319-72026-5_12.
[29] The Nature Conservancy and Environmental Finance. 2019. *Investing in Nature. Private Finance for Nature-Based Resilience*. London.
[30] Marsh & McLennan. 2018. Climate Resilience 2018 Handbook. Singapore; Smith, E. 2020. The numbers suggest the green investing "megatrend" is here to stay. https://www.cnbc.com/2020/02/14/esg-investing-numbers-suggest-green-investing-mega-trend-is-here.html.

International Development Actors Supporting Disaster Risk Reduction Finance

In addition to aspects that can help advance disaster risk reduction efforts by the public and private sector, it is also important to reflect on the strategic position of multilateral development banks and United Nations (UN) agencies in this regard (footnote 16). They (i) convene and intermediate between different public and private actors nationally and globally; (ii) offer a variety of financial, policy, technical, and capacity development products and services (Box 2.3); (iii) developed extensive experience with different structural and nonstructural interventions; and (iv) hold large and comparatively affordable resources that can be directed toward dedicated adaptation and risk reduction investments.

Box 2.3: Strengthening Transboundary Flood Risk Management in the Greater Mekong Subregion

The Integrated Disaster Risk Management (IDRM) Fund, administered by the Asian Development Bank (ADB) on behalf of the Government of Canada, provided a grant to support the Government of Viet Nam to develop more effective solutions to transboundary flood and drought risk in the country and across the border in Cambodia. The work included developing flood risk scenarios incorporating climate change projections. These flood risk scenarios supported decision-making around the type of hydraulic structures built for the Cuu Long delta. Following this, flood and flow management strategies for cross-border flooding were developed; these included preliminary evaluations of structural and nonstructural management strategies to reduce flood risk. The technical elements informed National Disaster Prevention and Control Plans for 50 communes in Tien Giang and Dong Thap districts, as well as 50 gender-sensitive community-based disaster risk management plans.

Additionally, another IDRM grant was provided to ADB's work with corridor towns in the Greater Mekong Subregion, including Viet Nam, Cambodia, and the Lao People's Democratic Republic (Lao PDR). It aimed to build capacity to develop resilient infrastructure to accommodate flood risk in key cities along the Mekong River corridor. The technical assistance led to three investment loans of $33 million to Cambodia, $100 million to Viet Nam, $137 million to the Lao PDR to support measures including (i) improved drainage and road systems; (ii) improved wastewater and stormwater systems, as well as solid waste management; (iii) improved flood management through land management, urban parks, and recreation spaces; (iv) riverbank stabilization works; and (v) community awareness campaigns on environmental sustainability and practices.

Ultimately, the IDRM Fund's support informed resilient infrastructure design and ensuing delivery, as well as knowledge sharing among experts, communities, and governments across the participating cities and countries.

Source: ADB. 2018. *Integrated Disaster Risk Management Fund – Annual Report*. Manila.

Multilateral development banks and UN agencies have reformed their approaches for mainstreaming disaster risk reduction across their sectors and operations—a process that is still ongoing—as the understanding and sophistication of corresponding solutions is evolving in partnership with government counterparts and consulting services and research providers (Box 2.4).[31] Through their country engagement strategies, multilateral development banks and UN organizations partner with governments to define the longer-term strategic direction of their relationship, evaluating the effectiveness, and derive learning from previous programs, identifying their organization's value-add to a country's broader development cooperation ecosystem; and engaging with

---

[31] World Bank. 2012. *Disaster Risk Management and Multilateral Development Banks. An Overview*. Washington, DC.

Box 2.4: Progress and Lessons from ADB's 2004 Disaster and Emergency Assistance Policy

As a key multilateral development bank in Asia and the Pacific, the Asian Development Bank (ADB) has consistently sought to address the significant challenges to poverty reduction and sustainable development posed by disasters and emergencies, as guided by its 2004 Disaster and Emergency Assistance Policy (DEAP). The DEAP covers ADB's overarching approach to disasters and emergencies including risk reduction, preparedness, recovery, and reconstruction, while also establishing the emergency assistance loan (EAL) modality. Over the life span of the DEAP, ADB has seen considerable growth in projects that embedded disaster risk reduction (from 23 projects in 1999–2003 to 177 projects in 2014–2018), increase in stand-alone disaster risk reduction projects (from 5 projects 1999–2003 to 10 projects in 2014–2018), provided support to 35 health security projects to address pandemic risk, and approved 40 EALs totaling $6.6 billion.

To inform country partnership strategies, a disaster risk management guidance note and informal disaster risk management country notes have been prepared to increase the consideration of disaster risk in ADB's strategic collaboration with developing member countries. This helped to include strategic or thematic (sub) priorities on disaster risk into 18 country partnership strategies by 2018 (over just 2 in 2008). Since the 2004 DEAP, ADB has also developed (i) a new loan modality on contingent disaster financing; (ii) set-asides in the Asian Development Fund for a Disaster Response Facility, the Disaster Risk Reduction financing mechanism, and for regional health security; (iii) a special fund for post-disaster relief (Asia Pacific Disaster Response Fund); (iv) trust fund resources for disaster risk management and health security; and (v) disaster insurance products and strengthening of the related enabling environment.

Learning from the 2004 DEAP implementation, areas for further enhancement have been identified, including (i) strengthening strategic guidance on ADB's overarching approach to disasters and emergencies, especially for risk reduction; (ii) ensuring careful consideration of disaster risk in project design and implementation; and (iii) achieving tailor-made resilience solutions as per individual country context.

Sources: ADB. 2017. *Disaster Risk Management and Country Partnership Strategies. A Practical Guide.* Manila.
ADB. 2019. *Review of the 2004 Disaster and Emergency Assistance Policy.* Manila.

civil society and the private sector to support new alliances in reducing disaster risks.[32] Such new alliances are important for developing countries—particular low-income ones—if they can identify and define their finance needs for disaster risk reduction and provide a holistic approach and platform—such as through integrated national financing frameworks—for other actors, such as bilateral assistance, to contribute to the implementation of development agendas (footnote 16).

Defining clear partnership strategies between international development organizations and national governments helps to outline policy priorities and related investment needs from a demand side. Besides the typical engagement of finance ministries, the involvement of other sector ministries can inform early-stage programming and project scoping to ensure understanding and implementation readiness later on. Clear partnership strategies also support a more effective coordination of efforts between development actors and a correspondingly more targeted use of their resources for specific action areas.

Multilateral development banks' country partnership strategies can help to move resilience from a cross-cutting issue to a priority area for development where this aligns with governments' development agenda focus (footnote 22). This can then allow for investments in resilient infrastructure to be accompanied by targeted investments that directly build systemic resilience through both policies and projects.

---

[32]   World Bank. 2018. *IBRD/IDA/IFC/MIGA Guidance: Country Engagement.* Washington, DC.; United Nations. 2019. *United Nations Sustainable Development Cooperation Framework. Internal Guidance.* New York.; ADB. 2017. *Disaster Risk Management and Country Partnership Strategies. A Practical Guide.* Manila.

3 Conceptualizing Disaster Risk Reduction Finance

Approaches to Disaster Risk Reduction Finance

There are broadly three ways entities—particularly those in the public sector—can approach disaster risk reduction finance.[33] While the three options described below focus on the national level, similar approaches are found at the subnational level, for instance in provincial or city governments, or private sector agencies and utilities with corresponding authority over disaster risk management functions and resources in particular sectors.

Disaster risk reduction finance through investment projects. In this option, funding is secured for the planning and implementation of a concrete disaster risk reduction measure (which can include both structural and nonstructural features). The advantage of a stand-alone disaster risk reduction project lies in its specificity, which allows to link the funding to clear implementable measures over a defined time frame. It can, therefore, be a good option in contexts, where the institutionalization of disaster risk reduction or disaster risk management is still limited. In order to have positive impacts beyond a particular (spatial) area, such projects should preferably be linked to complementary nonstructural measures that could, for instance, target reforms to existing policies or regulations and build capacities in executing and implementing agencies. This is illustrated by the support provided by the ADB's Integrated Disaster Risk Management Fund to governments in Southeast Asia (see Box 1.2). The ability to showcase achievements in a shorter time frame through individually financed disaster risk reduction projects can help build further buy-in from stakeholders and decision-makers for more comprehensive and long-term disaster risk reduction efforts, which link to the following two finance approaches.

Disaster risk reduction finance through dedicated funds.
A second option for financing disaster risk reduction is through a dedicated fund as exemplified by Pakistan's 2018-established National Disaster Risk Management Fund to increase the country's resilience to extreme weather and geophysical disasters (Box 2.1; also see Appendix 4 for the example of Mexico's Natural Disaster Prevention Fund). In this case, disaster risk reduction is put comparatively high on the overall political agenda and addressed in a more programmatic fashion. This allows different departments or government entities (at national and subnational levels) to apply for and/or be allocated specific resources from the dedicated fund based on a set of eligibility criteria. When designing such criteria, it is important to avoid perverse incentives

> **TOP TIP**
>
> There is no single right approach to disaster risk reduction finance. Tailor the approach to a specific country context and adjust it as lessons are learned through implementation.

---

[33] Jackson, D. 2011. Effective Financial Mechanisms at the National and Local Level for Disaster Risk Reduction. Paper Written for the Mid Term Review of the UNISDR Hyogo Framework for Action. New York: United Nations Capital Development Fund; Kellet, J., A. Caravani, and F. Pichon. 2014. *Financing Disaster Risk Reduction: Towards a Coherent and Comprehensive Approach*. London: ODI.

whereby sectoral departments would reduce their own ('normal') budget allocation to related investment or maintenance activities and simply replace those with resources that were meant to be "additional". [34]

A dedicated disaster risk reduction fund can also come with a mandatory contribution of a share of its fund from different departments. Such a fund would usually be managed by a dedicated unit, for instance, a national disaster risk management committee. One example is the National Resilience Taskforce within the Government of Australia's Department of Home Affairs, which functions as the coordinating body to execute the National Disaster Risk Reduction Framework, a 5-year, $90 million funding package for disaster reduction initiatives across Australia. [35]

Disaster risk reduction finance through budget line. A third option is the funding of disaster risk reduction as a budget line within sector department budgets (footnote 17). The budget line may be served directly through allocation from the national government and/or through mandatory contributions or policy-directed allocations by the concerned departments. As a dedicated budget line, disaster risk reduction would have to meet specific requirements or match defined criteria for spending, and form part of a department's works program or resource envelope for further distribution to recipients (e.g., local governments or regional development agencies, private sector entities, or households). Examples can be found in the Philippines' National Disaster Risk Reduction and Management Framework (Box 1.1) and in Costa Rica's National Risk Management. System (SNPRAE) (Appendix 4), whereby disaster risk is incorporated into all state and local budgets and programs through a mixed-model approach with stand-alone financing and sector ministries' budget surplus contribution.

Box 3: Reducing Disaster Risk in Pakistan with a National Disaster Risk Management Fund

Pakistan is vulnerable to a range of climate and disaster risks that can be acute (e.g., earthquakes, floods, landslides) and chronic (e.g., droughts and changing rainfall patterns). As a result, Pakistan, in partnership with the Asian Development Bank (ADB), established in May 2018 a National Disaster Risk Management Fund (NDRMF) to increase the country's resilience to extreme weather and geophysical disasters. Aligned with the National Disaster Management Plan 2012–2022 and the Draft National Flood Protection Plan IV 2016–2026, the NDRMF aims to reduce the socioeconomic and fiscal impacts of natural hazards and climate change by increasing institutional and physical capacities of public sector entities (federal and provincial government departments; special authorities; public academia) and nonpublic sector entities (UN, nongovernment organizations, civil society organizations, and nonpublic academia).

The Fund acts as a nonprofit financial intermediary, whose aim is to prioritize and finance investments that reduce disaster risk. The Fund initially started with a $200 million grant from ADB and is now supported by multiple donors. Previously, Pakistan lacked a funding window to coordinate disaster risk reduction efforts; therefore, the NDRMF is a major step toward integrating disaster risk reduction across sectors and institutional levels. The NDRMF finances up to 70% of the cost of eligible projects and, additionally, is working to transfer residual risks through insurance arrangements.

Sources: ADB. 2018. *Pakistan National Disaster Risk Management Fund*. https://www.adb.org/projects/50316-001/main. ADB. 2018. *Pakistan: National Disaster Risk Management Fund*. Manila. https://www.adb.org/sites/default/files/project-document/212811/50316-001-pam.pdf.

---

[34]   UNDRR. 2019. *Global Assessment Report on Disaster Risk Reduction*. Geneva; Resch, E. et al. 2018. *Mainstreaming, Accessing and Institutionalising Finance for Climate Change Adaptation. Action on Climate Today Learning Paper*. Oxford: Oxford Policy Management; Kellet, J., A. Caravani, and F. Pichon. 2014. *Financing Disaster Risk Reduction: Towards a Coherent and Comprehensive Approach*. London: ODI.
[35]   Department of Home Affairs. 2018. National Disaster Risk Reduction Framework. Brisbane.

Types of Disaster Risk Reduction Finance

Resource allocation for disaster risk reduction comes in two expenditure types: recurrent and capital. It can be spent on physical and nonphysical goods and services (Figure 3.1).[36]

Recurrent (operational) expenditures. Recurrent expenditures can be classified into two different types of expenditures. Firstly, goods and raw materials are purchased as inputs required to ensure the continued functioning and servicing of existing infrastructure and other assets that provide disaster risk reduction functions. For example, the sustainable urban drainage system of a city may include bioswales for gathering and filtering of stormwater and may require exchange of certain soil types or plants are part of its annual maintenance.

Secondly, expenditures for operations and services pay for the daily operation and maintenance activities carried out by government staff or contractors. Using the same example of the bioswale maintenance, service expenditures would include the costs for hiring a green engineering firm to undertake the maintenance work.

Together, those recurrent expenditures make previous investments into disaster risk reduction assets "pay off" by ensuring their effective operation and performance to expected standards.

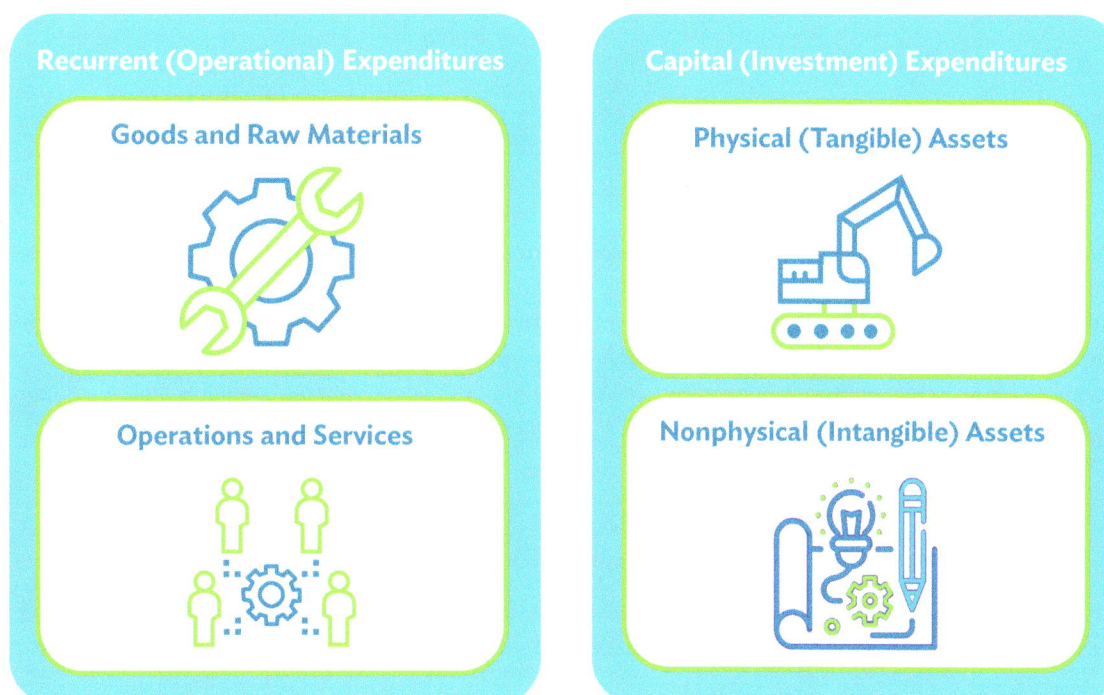

Figure 3.1: Types and Classification of Budgetary Resource Allocation

Source: Author.

36   Jackson, D. 2011. *Effective Financial Mechanisms at the National and Local Level for Disaster Risk Reduction.* Paper Written for the Mid Term Review of the UNISDR Hyogo Framework for Action. New York: United Nations Capital Development Fund; Kellet, J., A. Caravani, and F. Pichon. 2014. *Financing Disaster Risk Reduction: Towards a Coherent and Comprehensive Approach.* London: ODI.

> **TOP TIP**
>
> Disaster risk reduction is more than the infrastructure built. It requires a comprehensive package of "hard" and "soft" measures to reduce risk, capacitate people, and increase the resilience of communities and infrastructure assets.

Capital (investment) expenditures. Similarly, capital expenditures can also be classified into physical and nonphysical elements. Physical capital investments concern tangible disaster risk reduction assets. A classic example would be the investment into the construction of a new seawall protecting a low-lying settlement from coastal flooding.

Nonphysical capital investment, on the other hand, relates to intangible assets. In the case of the seawall investment, such intangible asset expenditure could concern the purchasing of latest weather data or modeling software to be able to better understand high-wave events, which can help to inform decisions on evacuating people from certain areas.

Typically, capital investments into physical assets are the primary focus in disaster risk reduction spending, as well as generally in public expenditure frameworks. However, it is important that such investments have a dedicated budget allocation for operations and maintenance, as well as skilled staff or contractors to properly operate and maintain the assets, otherwise the physical infrastructure ends up not functioning effectively or deteriorating before the estimated end of its lifetime.

Scoping and Selecting Instruments for Financing Disaster Risk Reduction

Before presenting different instruments for financing disaster risk reduction, a classification of nine criteria is offered that can be used in the identification, evaluation, and decision for or against a particular finance instrument for disaster risk reduction (Figure 3.2; see Appendix 3 for a detailed explanation).[37] Such criteria can help to screen the landscape of available instruments and better understand where each one's advantages and risks lie. Due to the varied and often interlinking nature of project or investment risks, financing instruments (described in Chapter 4) often need to be jointly deployed in the implementation of different structural and nonstructural measures. Such packaging of different types of finance—sometimes by using tailored finance vehicles—is a common approach to allow different finance type providers with different risk appetites to join together for an investment. Examples are wide-ranging from public–private partnerships and municipal development funds to investment funds, securitized products, and financing facilities, as further presented in the succeeding chapter.

---

[37]   ADB. 2019. *The Enabling Environment for Disaster Risk Financing in Fiji. Country Diagnostics Assessment.* Manila; UNESCAP. 2019. *The Future of Asian and Pacific cities. Transformative Pathways Towards Sustainable Urban Development.* Bangkok; World Bank. 2016. *Disaster Risk Finance as a Tool for Development. A Summary of Findings from the Disaster Risk Finance Impact Analytics Project.* Washington, DC.

Figure 3.2: Assessment Criteria for Disaster Risk Reduction Finance Instruments

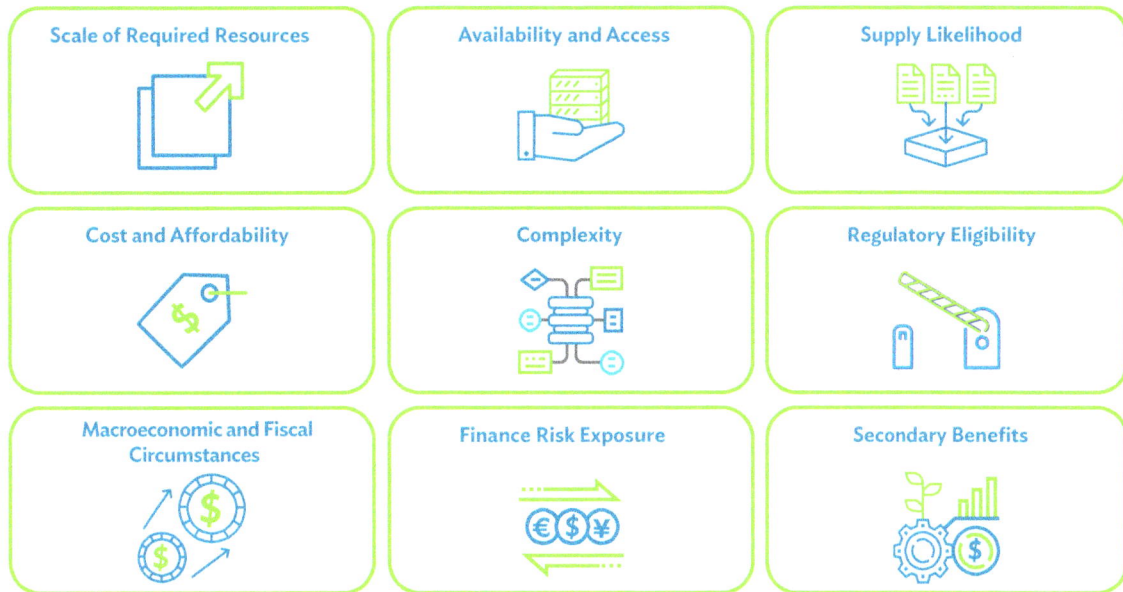

Scale of Required Resources	Availability and Access	Supply Likelihood
Cost and Affordability	Complexity	Regulatory Eligibility
Macroeconomic and Fiscal Circumstances	Finance Risk Exposure	Secondary Benefits

Source: Author.

4 Instruments for Financing Disaster Risk Reduction

This chapter provides an overview of instruments to finance structural and nonstructural disaster risk reduction measures. The instruments are broadly categorized into (Figure 4.1):

Own-source revenues are the resources that an entity, such as a provincial government, can generate through its own processes, typically from taxes and non-tax sources, such as tariffs, fees, charges, fines, sales, and leases.

Intergovernmental grants and transfers usually come from upper-level governments and international development partners through earmarked grants (for particular purposes) and unconditional (non-earmarked) grants, as well as subsidies.

Debt-type finance is borrowed capital and primarily comes from loans (which can be market-based or concessional and are provided by development partners and commercial lenders) and bonds (which are usually issued by firms or governments and can be traded in the market).

Equity-type finance are listed (in the stock exchange) or unlisted (privately held) ownership shares in an investment, whereby the "profit" does not usually come from fixed and regular interest payments as in the case of

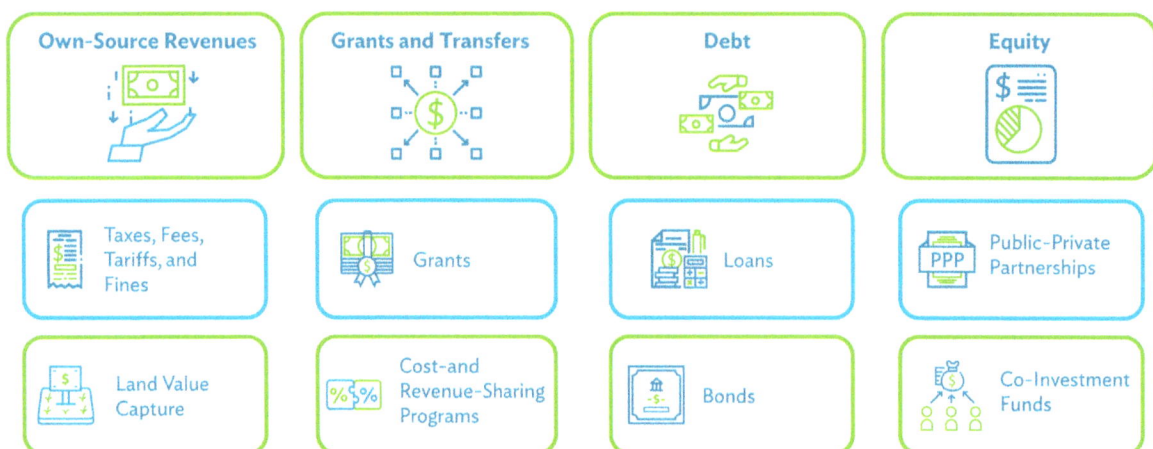

Figure 4.1: Categories and Examples of Finance Instruments for Disaster Risk Reduction

Own-Source Revenues	Grants and Transfers	Debt	Equity
Taxes, Fees, Tariffs, and Fines	Grants	Loans	Public-Private Partnerships
Land Value Capture	Cost-and Revenue-Sharing Programs	Bonds	Co-Investment Funds

Note: The examples given in this figure are not exhaustive. There are many other instruments and mechanisms under each of the four categories. Also see: C40 Cities Finance Facility. 2017. *Explainer: How to Finance Urban Infrastructure*. London (C40/GIZ).
Source: Author.

most debt-type finance, but from variable and less regular dividends. Due to the higher risk profile of equity-type finance in contrast to debt-type finance, equity-type finance bears the chance of higher returns, as well as losses.

The packaging of different types of finance into **tailored finance vehicles** is a common approach to allow different finance type providers with different risk appetites to join together for an investment. Examples are wide-ranging from public–private partnerships and municipal development funds to investment funds, securitized products, and financing facilities (see Chapter 3).

Own-Source Revenues

Own-source revenues from **taxes, fees, tariffs, and fines** can form a core element of governments' financing of disaster risk reduction. If designed effectively, they give incentive to disaster risk reduction actions by public sector entities, the private sector, households, and individuals. One own-source revenue instrument to highlight is **land value capture**, as it provides six mechanisms for governments to finance disaster risk reduction alongside land development.[38] Through (i) the strategic sale or lease of public land, (ii) development charges to investors, (iii) the sale of development rights or density credits, (iv) land pooling or readjustment, (v) betterment levies, and (vi) tax increment financing, land value capture offers the opportunity to strategically direct development to less disaster-prone areas, share costs for disaster-mitigating infrastructure, and provide incentives for others to invest in disaster risk-reducing measures (see Appendix 5 for further details on each mechanism). Essentially, the public sector has a range of nonfinancial tools at hand to indirectly advance disaster risk reduction, as illustrated in Figure 4.2 and further elaborated in Appendix 6.[39]

> **TOP TIP**
>
> Empower and incentivize subnational governments to exhaust own-source revenues to finance both recurrent and capital expenditures for disaster risk reduction.

Figure 4.2: Public Sector Nonfinancial Tools for Disaster Risk Reduction

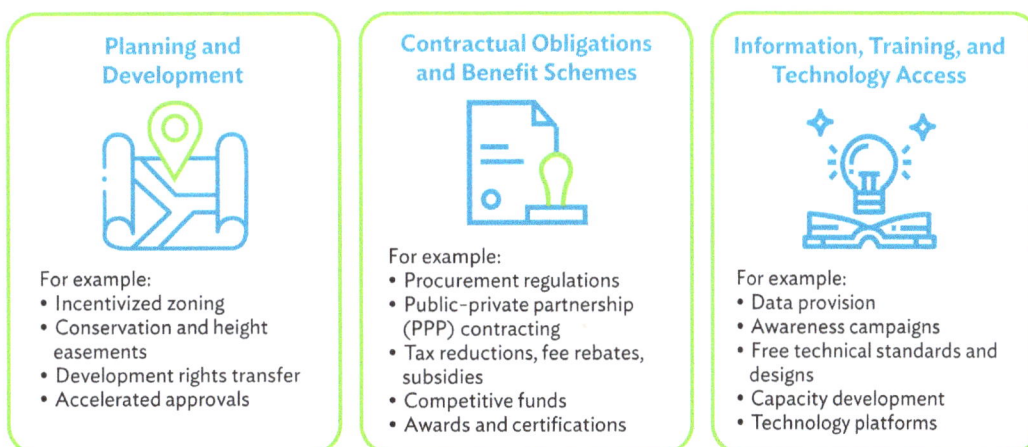

Planning and Development

For example:
- Incentivized zoning
- Conservation and height easements
- Development rights transfer
- Accelerated approvals

Contractual Obligations and Benefit Schemes

For example:
- Procurement regulations
- Public-private partnership (PPP) contracting
- Tax reductions, fee rebates, subsidies
- Competitive funds
- Awards and certifications

Information, Training, and Technology Access

For example:
- Data provision
- Awareness campaigns
- Free technical standards and designs
- Capacity development
- Technology platforms

Source: Author.

38   World Bank. 2018. *Land Value Capture. Investment in Infrastructure.* Washington, DC.
39   ADB. 2016. *Incentives for Reducing Disaster Risk in Urban Areas. Experiences from Da Nang (Viet Nam), Kathmandu Valley (Nepal), and Naga City (Philippines).* Manila; Micale, V., B. Tonkonogy, and F. Mazza. 2018. *Understanding and Increasing Finance for Climate Adaptation in Developing Countries.* San Francisco: Climate Policy Initiative and Adelphi.

Grant and Transfer Instruments

Grants and transfers can go a long way in incentivizing disaster risk reduction measures at national and subnational levels (footnote 11). In general, they can come from central government, multilateral and bilateral development banks and funds, and nongovernment organizations (e.g., philanthropies) (Figure 3.2).

One allocation mechanism is **earmarked grants** that directly—and sometimes fully—finance disaster risk reduction projects. Related to this are **top-up (incremental) grants** in addition to base funding. Such grants allow for instance additional hazard aspects to be assessed and incorporated into the design of infrastructure or other assets. Another approach is to structure **performance-based or conditional grants** (Box 4.1). In this case, national departments or, more typically, subnational government entities only qualify for grant financing if they fulfill certain criteria, for instance, having a disaster risk reduction plan in place before being eligible for capital investment budget.

Box 4.1: Nepal's Minimum Conditions and Performance Measures

The Government of Nepal incentivizes disaster risk reduction through the use of Minimum Conditions and Performance Grants. Through this system, local governments and developers are eligible to receive grant funding that is adjusted annually based on how their plans score across a range of criteria, including requirements for emergency services and disaster management. They receive payouts upon successfully illustrating that they have maintained compliance. Additionally, the top six performing municipalities receive varying amounts of cash awards. This has led to a range of disaster management activities, including the establishment of disaster management committees at the ward level throughout Kathmandu Valley, increasing budgets to spread public awareness of hazards, and establishing local networks for knowledge sharing of disaster preparedness. This complements Nepal's Local Adaptation Plans of Action (LAPAs), which are developed by local governments and aim to take a bottom-up approach to reducing vulnerability. The Minimum Conditions and Performance Grants can thus support the LAPAs by providing potential funding for programs that reduce vulnerability.

Sources: ADB. 2016. *Incentives for Reducing Disaster Risk in Urban Areas. Experiences from Da Nang (Viet Nam), Kathmandu Valley (Nepal), and Naga City (Philippines).* Manila.
Chan, C. and N. Amerasinghe. 2018. *Deploying Adaptation Finance for Maximum Impact. Commentary.* Washington DC: World Resources Institute.

TOP TIP

Every group contributing some of its own financial resources to disaster risk reduction efforts can ensure awareness, buy-in, and joint efforts toward successful implementation.

In a similar way, **competitive grant funds** allow access to additional grant financing from government for those proposed projects or initiatives that align best with the fund's disaster risk reduction objectives. An advantage of such a fund is that it usually outlines its intended outcomes without dictating the use of specific solutions, methods, or tools. This creates space for stakeholders' local knowledge to tailor project design to their specific context. However, larger entities with more capacity often find it easier to access such funds, while constrained administrations may simply not have the personnel or time to consider these funding avenues.

Cost-sharing programs are another effective method for disaster risk reduction finance, as they require cofinancing from the recipient entity. This approach is often used in inter-governmental grants from the central to the subnational government, or in programs by supranational unions, such as the European Union, to allow a more flexible financing according to local investment needs. It can also help to strengthen ownership and commitment to disaster risk reduction measures by receiving entities as they are dedicating part of their own money to the effort.

> ### Box 4.2: Strengthening Resilience by Supporting Grassroots, Women-Led Solutions
>
> Established by the Government of Canada and the Asian Development Bank to advance proactive integrated disaster risk management measures on a regional basis, the Integrated Disaster Risk Reduction Management Fund supported Indonesia, the Philippines, and Viet Nam through the project "Closing the Gap: Empowering Women to Link Community Resilience Priorities to Decentralized Development." This project aimed to support resilience and reduce disaster risk by building the capacity of community-based women organizations in both rural and urban areas to engage with local authorities on accessing local development funds to support community-level disaster risk reduction needs. Where local governments have specific funds earmarked for disaster risk reduction, the underlying mechanism helped community-based organizations and women to assess disaster risk in a participatory manner. This, in turn, supported decentralized decision-making to ensure disaster risk reduction efforts were tailored to the local context, avoiding the pitfalls of prescriptive or "one-size fits all" approaches.
>
> Source: ADB. 2017. *Integrated Disaster Risk Management Fund – Annual Report.* Manila.

Debt Instruments

In country settings where international and national development banks are allowed and tasked to provide (concessional) debt for national and subnational disaster risk reduction investments, **loans** can play a crucial role.[40] To advance related projects, there are two options: (i) **(concessional) loan facilities/funds** that are exclusively available to dedicated disaster risk reduction investments, and (ii) **incentivized (discounted) lending rates** for investments that fulfill minimum resilience requirements. Following the efforts of multilateral development banks to build resilience considerations into development project lending, many national development banks are taking similar steps, including efforts to future-proof their portfolios by prioritizing lending to projects that have incorporated climate and disaster-resilient designs and/or are not detrimental to other resilience efforts. This is illustrated by recent efforts of, for instance, PT Sarana Multi Infrastruktur in Indonesia or İller Bankası Anonim Şirketi (Ilbank) in Turkey. However, corresponding initiatives and programs require further capacity development to strengthen understanding, planning, design, implementation, and monitoring of disaster risk reduction projects.[41]

A second major form of debt-financing is through **bonds**. As an investment category, bonds have evolved over the past 3 decades, now featuring, for example, municipal bonds (linked to projects, proceeds, general obligations, social impact, and environmental performance), corporate bonds (linked for instance to municipal utility companies), and Sharia-compliant *sukuk-type* bonds (in alignment with Islamic banking principles). More specifically, the bond market has evolved and is adapting to the needs of resilience-focused investments, as the examples below illustrate.[42]

Environmental impact bonds. Similar to their "sister" instrument of social impact bonds, environmental impact bonds (EIBs) are an innovative financing tool that uses a "pay for success" approach to provide up-front capital from private investors for environmental projects, either to pilot a new approach whose performance is viewed as uncertain or to scale-up a solution that has been successfully tested (footnote 29). EIBs are most often linked to the work of infrastructure utility companies working, for instance, in the water sector, as illustrated by the DC Water Environmental Impact Bond (Appendix 7). The DC Water EIB provided funding to manage

---

[40] C40 Cities Finance Facility. 2017. *Explainer: How to Finance Urban Infrastructure.* London: C40/GIZ.
[41] ADB. 2017. Disaster Risk Assessment for Project Preparation. A Practical Guide. Manila.
[42] Other emerging niche bonds targeted at diaspora communities of a country are migrant disaster risk insurance bonds, diaspora reconstruction or catastrophe bonds, as well as community disaster risk reduction funds. ADB. 2013. Investing in Resilience. *Ensuring a Disaster-Resistant Future.* Manila.

stormwater runoff and improve local water quality through the construction of green infrastructure, whereby the bond was used to fund the construction, while proceed payments were dependent on certain performance metrics of the chosen environmental intervention.[43] To succeed, investors promote a very close relationship between engaged parties and to intermediate additional technical support to ensure the effectiveness of a project, which would help in meeting profitability margins.

Green and resilience bonds. The green bond market has experienced a phenomenal growth, although one should caution that in 2018, still less than 0.2% of all bonds issued were green bonds, and within the green bonds, just 3%–5% could be linked to climate resilience efforts. Nevertheless, green bonds for resilience investments are slowly emerging (Box 4.3 and Appendix 7).[44] In principal, a bond linked to disaster risk reduction infrastructure would function by taking a particular infrastructure asset (or a pool of several assets, see below under aggregation) and either identifying a revenue stream directly from the asset to serve the bond proceed payments, or to ensure regular revenue flow from the infrastructure asset's owner.

As a specialized instrument, a **resilience bond** uses features of a catastrophe bond in terms of insurance premiums linked to disaster events (not) happening (which is used in disaster risk financing, see Appendix 9). However, it works with two scenarios: one which assumes the investment area without any resilience investment (and thus more vulnerable to disaster event impacts) and one where the resilience investment makes the investment area less vulnerable, thereby reducing potential losses. This estimated difference in losses becomes the "resilience rebate" that supports the funding of structural and nonstructural resilience projects.[45]

TOP TIP

Inviting the private sector to devise ways to combine different finance instruments and sources for resilient investments has resulted in innovative ways of realizing projects that the public sector alone would have not been able to finance.

For example, the project owner, e.g., the municipal government, could fund upgrading projects in a previously flood-prone neighborhood through a resilience bond whereby it saves on catastrophe insurance premium payments which, in turn, provides funding for resilience-strengthening measures. Linking this to the application of betterment levies in the neighborhood could also provide for additional revenues to serve the bond proceed payments under the premise that the reduction of flood risk in the neighborhood results in an increase in property values and a corresponding growth in property taxes (also see Appendix 5).

For such resilience bonds to find sufficient interested investors and to scale-up over the coming years, broadly agreed standards and metrics are important. Following the 2015 Standard and Certification Scheme for Green Bonds, the Climate Bonds Initiative published its first framework to assess climate resilience investments in 2019 (footnote 27). This came as a response to green bonds being predominantly focused on climate mitigation assets, while the adaptation field was lacking a clear taxonomy and methodology to make its investments fit green bond instruments and structures.

SDG bonds. Bonds linked to the Sustainable Development Goals (SDGs) are a new form of the bond instrument, where a coupon payment to investors is determined by the issuer's performance against certain targets within the SDGs (footnote 27). This is of interest to disaster risk reduction beyond purely environmental performance measures. For example, nature-based solutions are a key contributor to resilience to climate-

[43]   Goldman Sachs. 2016. *Fact Sheet: DC Water Environmental Impact Bond.*
[44]   Climate Bonds Initiative. 2019. *Climate Resilience Principles. A Framework for Assessing Climate Resilience Investments.* London; RMS for DFID. 2018. *Financial Instruments for Resilient Infrastructure. Technical Report.* London.
[45]   Vaijhala, S. and J. Rhodes. 2018. *Resilience Bonds: A Business-Model for Resilient Infrastructure. Field Actions Science Reports Special Issue* 18. pp. 58–63; Refocus. 2017. *Leveraging Catastrophe Bonds. As a Mechanism for Resilience Infrastructure Project Finance.* http://www.refocuspartners.com/wp-content/uploads/2017/02/RE.bound-Program-Report-December-2015.pdf.

related disasters (e.g., acting as buffers for floodwater and mediating extreme heat events) and investments in this space are proliferating, which will have knock-on effects for disaster risk reduction-linked bond issuance.[46] Although the quantification before bond issuance and the monitoring during the implementation time frame are challenging, SDG bonds reflect the cross-sector nature of disaster risk reduction and also allow for resilience to be incorporated into a wider bundle of economic, social, and environmental objectives under a single SDG bond. Dutch NWB Bank has exemplified this through its 2017 SDG Housing Bond, where proceeds are invested into social housing associations with performance evaluated against 45 indicators aligned with 8 SDGs, including investments into environmentally and socially resilient community services and neighborhood improvements.[47]

Box 4.3: Fiji as First Developing Country to Issue Green Bond

Fiji comprises 300 low-lying volcanic islands and atolls which are at high risk from cyclones and flooding events. Furthermore, nearly 20% of the population faces displacement due to climate change by 2050. Fiji incurred economic losses comparable to one-third of its annual gross domestic product due to the impacts of Tropical Cyclone Winston in 2016. Following this, Fiji issued its first sovereign green bond to support climate change mitigation and adaptation in 2017, raising $50 million—with its first tranche oversubscribed by more than double the original amount. Fiji was the first developing country to issue a green bond. Its green bond will fund projects with clear environmental and social benefits, including renewable energy investments, restoring native trees, building more resilient schools, and supporting the country to meet its commitment to the Paris Agreement.

Sources: COP23. 2017. *Fiji's Green Bond.* https://cop23.com.fj/fiji-green-bond/#:~:text=In%20October%202017%2C%20 Fiji%20became,climate%20change%20mitigation%20and%20adaption.
International Finance Corporation. 2017. *A Green Bond to Help Fiji Secure a Greener Future.* https://www.ifc.org/wps/wcm/connect/ news_ext_content/ifc_external_corporate_site/news+and+events/news/cm-stories/fiji-green-bond-for-a-greener-future.

Equity Instruments

While debt and grant financing play a dominant role in exclusively publicly funded investments, equity-type finance is mostly related to public sector shares in **public-private partnerships** or public sector shares in **utilities and other infrastructure assets** that can attract capital market investment. Good practice in integrating disaster risk management into public-private partnerships can be found for instance in Japan (Box 4.4).

Another instrument that can play a role in disaster risk reduction finance is **viability gap funding** by the public sector (or international donors, such as through the Technical Assistance Facility of the Private Infrastructure Development Group). Typically found in public–private partnerships, it has been applied to close the gap for emerging resilience technology to allow private sector to invest in those risk layers of an asset that match their investment horizon and risk-return profile, while the public sector takes on the remaining shares and/or finances the up-front project preparation costs (footnote 40).

This is linked to an evolving engagement of the private sector in financing resilient infrastructure and disaster risk reduction projects.[48] There is an increasing interest of the private sector and capital markets to tailor their finance instruments to the specific needs of financing disaster risk reduction with a private sector profit objective in mind.

---

[46]   Maxwell, Dorothy. 2017. Valuing Natural Capital: Future Proofing Business and Finance. Abingdon: Routledge.
[47]   NWB Bank. 2019. SDG Housing Bonds. Sustainable Indicator Report 2019. The Hague.
[48]   United Nations. 2008. *Private Sector Activities in Disaster Risk Reduction. Good Practices and Lessons Learned.* Bonn.

Box 4.4: Integrating Disaster Risk Management in Public–Private Partnerships in Japan

In the context of disaster risks, public–private partnerships (PPPs) can be looked at in terms of conducive policy and legal frameworks, contracting and disaster risk allocation, procurement, monitoring, and payment mechanisms, as well as insurance and reinsurance. The case of Japan provides valuable insights into all of these, with incentive mechanisms in the procurement playing a crucial role in advancing disaster risk reduction and improved disaster risk management in PPPs. Firstly, contractually mandating private operators to shoulder post-disaster responsibilities can encourage heightened attention to risk reduction measures being integrated into a project's proposed design and performance specifications. Secondly, requiring the inclusion of disaster risk management measures in tender submissions can allow for prioritizing proposals that would eventually result in reduced disaster risk of the PPP facility. Going beyond structural measures proposed for the design, such measures would also include "soft" interventions that provide for institutional arrangements that make disaster preparedness, response, and recovery more effective. Thirdly, the adjustment of availability payments can be used to compensate or penalize actual performance during a disaster event, for instance, in terms of structural damages to a facility or length of repair. Mechanisms like these have been applied, for instance, to PPPs for an astronomical observatory, a school meal supply center, and airports.

Source: World Bank. 2017. *Resilient Infrastructure Public–Private Partnerships (PPPs): Contracts and Procurement. The Case of Japan*. Washington, DC.

TOP TIP

Reach out to city networks and green finance platforms for advice on latest instruments, mechanisms, and potentially interested investors for disaster risk reduction, and to share lessons with other peers.

Co-investment funds have also been established as vehicles for direct investment in resilient livelihood and infrastructure projects, whereby public and private capital provide investment through debt and equity of different risk profiles (including, for instance, guarantee instruments such as subordinated debt in the form of mezzanine finance). Often, public participation acts as a driver and trust-builder for private sector participation in otherwise underfunded areas, particularly in terms of new technologies and approaches to adapt to disaster and climate change impacts (footnote 29).

Recognizing the challenges of "bankable" projects in this area, multilateral development banks and national governments have been developing investment vehicles that apply **blended finance**.[49] Based on well-designed investment vehicles that are supported and guaranteed by bilateral or multilateral development banks and sufficiently capitalized national governments, blended finance provides risk-matched entry and exit points for different investors (Box 4.5).

Besides those mixed public and private investment vehicles, there have also been important innovations in private sector finance for resilience investments in terms of **aggregation and securitization** (footnote 27). It addresses the challenge that some types of disaster risk reduction measures or projects may be of comparatively small size, which does not allow them to be placed in the bond market or as stand-alone equity that would attract sufficient interest from investors. Aggregation and securitization are also an interesting mechanism for entities, such as municipal governments, that only have limited assets to back up debt or debt-equity-based instruments toward capital market investors.

Aggregation allows for the bundling of several smaller-scale projects into an investment vehicle, which could then be (re)financed in the capital market through bonds and sale of equity shares. The bundling avoids project-by-project evaluation and pricing by individual investors, if the due diligence of the projects by the investment

49   ADB. 2017. *Catalyzing Green Finance. A Concept for Leveraging Blended Finance for Green Development*. Manila.

Box 4.5: Catalyzing Climate Finance with the Shandong Green Development Fund

The objective of the Shandong Green Development Fund (SGDF) is to implement an innovative, replicable and scalable form of cofinancing facility that will tap new funding sources, both public and private, leveraging catalyst concessional sources of finance for a pipeline of viable climate-resilient and low-emission investments. The SGDF will do this by (i) ensuring that the fund addresses priority climate impacts and vulnerabilities in Shandong, People's Republic of China; (ii) incorporating a project development facility to develop a pipeline of sustainable and replicable subprojects that will support project sponsors to achieve high levels of performance against Green Climate Fund (GCF) investment criteria; and (iii) leveraging private, institutional, and commercial (PIC) finance. Using a "cascade financing" approach, private financing will be leveraged at both the facility and project levels. The seed capital of $400 million from international financial institutions (including from the Asian Development Bank, French Development Agency AfD, German Development Bank KfW, and GCF), $360 million from public sources, and $740 million from private investors is expected to achieve a leverage ratio of 1:5 by cofinancing about $7.5 billion of climate-positive investment. Adaptation investment is to be at least 25% of SGDF's portfolio and the fund has developed a methodology for benchmarking portfolio composition against the priority sectors for adaptation interventions as defined by a climate vulnerability analysis—specifically coastal protection, flood control, water resilience, and greening or heat island—prioritized by numbers of people under threat.

Sources: ADB. 2019. *Report and Recommendation of the President to the Board of Directors. Proposed Loan People's Republic of China: Shandong Green Development Fund Project* (51194-001). Manila.
Jenny, H. et al. 2020. *Catalyzing Climate Finance with the Shandong Green Development Fund.* ADB Briefs: 144. Manila.

---

vehicle has been performed in a way that assures investors of the investability.[50] It also provides a platform for smaller entities to come together, spread financial and performance risk across several projects or assets, and benefit from the higher technical capacity within the joint investment vehicle. Typically, this mechanism can be found in municipal development funds that provide pooled financing or revolving funds for several municipal entities that, on their own, would often lack the financial and technical capacity and usually not be authorized to access capital markets.[51] A classic example is the Tamil Nadu Urban Development Fund in India, under which the Tamil Nadu Urban Flagship Investment Program features investments into priority water supply, sewerage, and drainage infrastructure focused on environmental sustainability, climate resilience, and urban livability.[52]

Securitization as a mechanism is often linked to aggregation (footnote 29). In this case, a bundle of small projects that previously did not provide any liquidity to their owners would become tradable in the capital market as asset-backed securities. Those securities would only attract investors if revenue flows can be ensured, either through the assets themselves (e.g., through user tariffs) or through the asset owners (e.g., through government budget allocations financed through property taxes), which back the security with **"resilient" collateral assets** (e.g., a portfolio of flood- and earthquake-resilient toll bridges). One such example is Beijing Enterprises Water Group, which issued a green asset-backed security on its water treatment plants that it operates for 16 municipalities in the People's Republic of China. The security is backed by the receivables from those water treatment services fee, with the proceeds being invested into nine infrastructure projects for water pollution prevention, water resource recycling, and water adaptation.[53]

An alternative version to this is **securitization with green use of proceeds**, which would relate to asset-backed securities that are not necessarily in themselves green or resilient, but whose proceeds will be invested into disaster risk reduction projects. Somewhat similar is the third type of **"synthetic securitization."** This basically frees up an issuer's balance sheet by transferring parts of assets' risk to an investor. This transfer provides

---

50   Chan, C. and N. 2018. *Deploying Adaptation Finance for Maximum Impact. Commentary.* Washington DC: World Resources Institute.
51   ADB. 2015. *Strengthening City Disaster Risk Financing in Viet Nam.* Manila.
52   Tamil Nadu Urban Infrastructure Financial Services Limited. 2019. Tamil Nadu Urban Development Fund. About Us. http://tnuifsl.com/tnudf.asp.
53   Climate Bonds Initiative. 2018. *Green Securitisation. Unlocking Finance for Small-Scale Low Carbon Projects.* Briefing Paper: March. London.

freed up capital for the issuer to invest into green or resilient projects, as happened with Credit Agricole's 2017 synthetic securitization of $3 billion of its infrastructure portfolio (of mostly non-green loans and "legacy assets") to increase its available capital for new green investments.[54]

International Development Finance

TOP TIP

Benefit from the knowledge in international development organizations for accessing global green and climate funds. Use the variety of project preparation facilities that provide grants and technical expertise for planning and designing disaster risk reduction projects that meet fund eligibility requirements.

UN agencies, multilateral development banks, and other international development organizations are well-placed to support disaster risk reduction financing and technical support (footnote 31). They cover a range of activities from initial technical assistance for risk assessments over project conceptualization and design through to construction and retrofitting of infrastructure, as well as disaster response, recovery, and reconstruction (Figure 4.3). In a nutshell, many of these organizations provide a **broad array of different financing instruments**, including, primarily, grants and (concessional) loans, as well as equity finance and risk mitigation for both the public and private sectors. Below, key instruments are presented that specifically support disaster risk reduction efforts in developing member countries.

Global funds. Global funds have been set up or include funding windows for climate adaptation and disaster risk reduction measures. Generally, these instruments facilitate financing to national implementing entities (e.g., national governments) and multilateral implementing entities (e.g., accredited UN organizations, multilateral development banks, nongovernment organizations, and businesses). Examples of global funds active in disaster risk reduction or disaster and climate resilience more broadly are the

Figure 4.3: International Development Organizations' Support to Disaster Risk Reduction

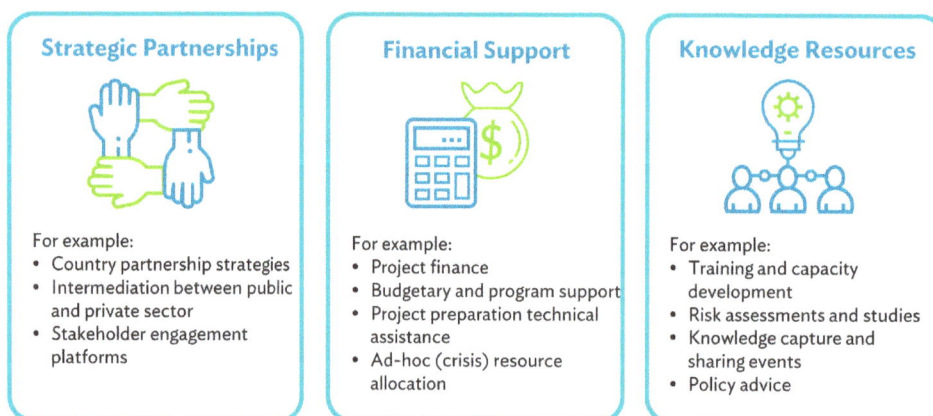

Strategic Partnerships

For example:
- Country partnership strategies
- Intermediation between public and private sector
- Stakeholder engagement platforms

Financial Support

For example:
- Project finance
- Budgetary and program support
- Project preparation technical assistance
- Ad-hoc (crisis) resource allocation

Knowledge Resources

For example:
- Training and capacity development
- Risk assessments and studies
- Knowledge capture and sharing events
- Policy advice

Source: Author.

54   Kidney, S. 2017. Deep-Dive: Green Synthetic Securitisation Deal: Frees USD 2bn of Capital for Green Investments - Crédit Agricole and Mariner Investment Group Take the Plunge. Climate Bonds Initiative: 13 March. https://www.climatebonds.net/2017/03/deep-dive-green-synthetic-securitisation-deal-frees-usd-2bn-capital-green-investments-cr%C3%A9dit.

Adaptation Fund and the Green Climate Fund (Appendix 8), as well as bilaterally initiated funds, such as the German Government's International Climate Initiative Fund (IKI Fund).[55]

Trust funds. There are several trust funds in the international development arena that were set up to focus on topics around disaster risk reduction, climate change adaptation, and environmental resilience. Examples of these are the Global Facility for Disaster Reduction and Recovery (GFDRR) under World Bank's management and the Urban Climate Change Resilience Trust Fund (UCCRTF) under ADB's management.[56]

Specialist mechanisms and programs. To make available additional dedicated resources to disaster risk reduction activities in developing member countries, multilateral development banks have devised specific financing mechanisms and programs, such as the Africa Disaster Risks Financing (ADRiFi) Program by the African Development Bank or the Green Cities Program by the European Bank for Reconstruction and Development. One example in Asia and the Pacific is the Asian Development Fund 12 Disaster Risk Reduction Financing Mechanism (Box 4.6).

Disaster Risk Financing and Insurance. Providing financing support for disaster response, recovery, and reconstruction, international finance institutions have also devised instruments such as contingent disaster finance

---

Box 4.6: Asian Development Fund 12 Disaster Risk Reduction Financing Mechanism

The changes over recent years and the potential for enhanced disaster risk reduction finance are exemplified in how the Asian Development Fund (ADF) grants of the Asian Development Bank (ADB) have evolved. The ADF was established in 1974 and provides grants and concessional loans to lower-income developing member countries of ADB. It supports development projects and programs for infrastructure, policy, and capacity development—including investments in disaster risk reduction.

A disaster risk reduction financing mechanism within the ADF was included in the 12th period (2017–2020). Initially, $164 million was allocated to the ADF disaster risk reduction financing mechanism, which was then increased to $195 million in 2019. The swift programming of the grants under the mechanism reflected the interest and efforts of both ADB and its developing member countries to pursue targeted disaster risk reduction activities. Through the process of programming the financing and devising its use in specific projects, awareness and opportunities around the topic could be raised among decision-makers.

One strategic area of a new thematic pool under ADF 13 focuses on grants for disaster risk reduction to developing member countries that struggle most with creditworthiness and low gross national income per capita. In detail, the ADF 13 thematic pool will support projects in the concessional assistance only developing member countries—group A countries, including International Development Association (IDA)-gap countries—and, on a very selective basis, group B countries. Priority will be given to fragile and conflict-affected situations and small island developing states. Eligible areas for support under the pool include grants for disaster risk reduction to incentivize government investment by providing concessional resources for (i) resilience projects that would otherwise not take place, (ii) for incorporating resilience components into projects, or—for group B countries—to strengthen resilience of the poorest and most vulnerable population by (i) piloting innovative resilience solutions, or (ii) leveraging additional (public and/or private) finance to strengthen resilience.

Sources: ADB. 2019. Supporting Disaster Risk Management: Disaster Risk Reduction Financing Mechanism and Disaster Response Facility. Asian Development Fund (ADF) ADF 12 Midterm Review Meeting: 27–28 February, Manila, Philippines. Manila; ADB. 2019. ADF 13 Thematic Pool. Manila; ADB. 2020. Implementation of the ADF 13 Thematic Pool of Grant Resources. Indicative Guidelines as of 7 May 2020. Manila.

---

55 Green Climate Fund. 2020. GCF 101: Project Funding. https://www.greenclimate.fund/gcf101/funding-projects/project-funding; Adaptation Fund. 2020. About the Adaptation Fund. https://www.adaptation-fund.org/about/; World Bank. 2020. Financial Intermediary Funds (FIFs): Adaptation Fund. https://fiftrustee.worldbank.org/en/about/unit/dfi/fiftrustee/fund-detail/adapt.
56 ADB. 2020. Urban Climate Change Resilience Trust Fund. https://www.adb.org/site/funds/funds/urban-climate-change-resilience-trust-fund; GFDRR. 2020. Global Facility for Disaster Reduction and Recovery. https://www.gfdrr.org/en/global-facility-disaster-reduction-and-recovery.

and emergency assistance grants and loans. In the case of high-impact disaster events with related repercussions on a country's fiscal system, they also offer restructuring and (in rare cases) loan cancellation options.[57] Multilateral development banks also support in the design of regional disaster risk insurance vehicles with technical expertise and intermediated access to the global reinsurance market.[58] One such example is the Pacific Catastrophe Risk Assessment and Financing Initiative (PCRAFI), which aims to reduce and manage disaster risk by providing robust modeling and assessment tools to improve the resilience of pacific island countries.[59] Although disaster risk financing is beyond the scope of this paper (see Appendix 9 for an overview), it is mentioned here, because some of its instruments are linked to policy reforms, institutional development, and proactive risk mitigation, which incentivize recipient governments to invest into disaster risk reduction (Box 4.7).[60]

Box 4.7: Developing Contingent Disaster Financing to Strengthen Disaster Preparedness

the Asian Development Bank (ADB) has developed contingent disaster financing (CDF), a new financing mechanism, which will provide a quick and flexible funding source to support disaster preparedness and response for ADB's developing member countries. The CDF covers typhoon, flood, earthquake, drought, and tsunami-triggered disasters. The key feature of the CDF is that the policy reforms and loan processing are implemented prior to the disaster event, and disbursement occurs following a triggering event.

The CDF builds on successful past programs including the ADB-financed Cook Islands Disaster Resilience Program. This program has provided the Government of the Cook Islands rapid access to financing resources to meet short-term, post-disaster recovery needs. The Cook Islands experiences periodic and major cyclones which have, in recent years, caused significant damage to infrastructure, the economy, and loss of life. These climatic events are set to increase with the worsening effects of climate change. The Resilience Program funding aims to support and facilitate the improvement of the national disaster risk management system by supporting better planning, response, and recovery from disaster events. As the funding is contingent, the government has to implement measures for improved disaster risk management governance, capacity development, resilience improvements to infrastructure assets, and expanded financing of disaster risk reduction.

Sources: ADB. 2016. Report and Recommendation of the President to the Board of Directors. Proposed Policy-Based Loan. Cook Islands: Disaster Resilience Program (50212-001). Manila.
ADB. 2019. Contingent Disaster Financing under Policy-Based Lending in Response to Natural Hazards. Policy Paper. Manila.

Programmatic Technical Assistance-to-Loan Support. Partly financed by some of the abovementioned funds, programs, and instruments, international development organizations have increasingly taken a more programmatic approach in uniting activities from disaster risk assessments and reduction through to post-disaster measures. The rationale is to build multiyear partnerships with national and subnational governments to assess, plan, and invest in disaster resilience to achieve reduced impacts and sustained economic and social development (Box 4.8).[61]

---

[57]   ADB. 2019. Contingent Disaster Financing under Policy-Based Lending in Response to Natural Hazards. Policy Paper. Manila; World Bank. 2015. *World Bank Group Development Solutions for Disaster Risk Finance*. Washington, DC.
[58]   World Bank. 2016. Towards a Regional Approach to Disaster Risk Finance in Asia. Discussion Paper. Washington, DC.
[59]   World Bank. 2015. *Pacific Catastrophe Risk Insurance Pilot. From Design to Implementation. Some Lessons Learned*. Washington, DC.
[60]   ADB. 2019. Contingent Disaster Financing under Policy-Based Lending in Response to Natural Hazards. Policy Paper. Manila.
[61]   See, for instance: ADB. 2018. ADB to Climate-Proof Nuku'alofa Electricity Network in Tonga. News Release: 18 June. Manila.

Box 4.8: Urban Climate Change Resilience Trust Fund's Programmatic Support to Cities

The Urban Climate Change Resilience Trust Fund (UCCRTF) is a $150 million multi-donor trust fund (2013–2021) administered by the Asian Development Bank (ADB) under the Urban Financing Partnership Facility. It provides support to medium-sized, rapidly growing cities to better integrate resilience into the planning and design of their infrastructure from strategy development to implementation. The fund also provides soft investments around institutional resilience capacity, as well as knowledge sharing and support in monitoring and evaluation.

Viet Nam is one of the ADB developing member countries that receive support from the UCCRTF for early-stage technical assistance through to loan implementation. From 2014 to 2015, Green City Action Plans were developed for three cities to mainstream climate change into urban development and investment prioritization. This engagement helped inform the $170 million ADB Secondary Green Cities Development Project (SGCDP). Its grant components are financed through the UCCRTF and the Global Environment Facility. The loan project aims to demonstrate economically competitive, environmentally sustainable, and socially inclusive development in the three cities to scale-up secondary green city development across Viet Nam.

Aiming to reduce disaster risk by mitigating flood risk and improving water infrastructure and services, the project is particularly looking at water-sensitive urban design (WSUD). This is an approach that integrates nature-based solutions within, or in place of, gray infrastructure to enhance water cycle management and reduce disaster risk. For example, in Vinh Yen, the project is financing 66 kilometers of drainage control and 45 hectares of new public green space. The project is upgrading 22 kilometers of drainage pipelines in Hue and will protect 6 kilometers of river embankments in Ha Giang. In addition, the UCCRTF grant contributes to community-led projects in Hue and Vinh Yen, as well as a sanitation revolving fund in Vinh Yen. WSUD capacity development support has also been provided alongside ADB's ongoing activities in Ho Chi Minh City.

The UCCRTF is also supporting capacity building and knowledge sharing through the Spatial Data Analysis Explorer (SPADE). Launched in 2018, SPADE hosts geospatial information for a growing number of cities on its cloud-based platform. It is used as a tool to inform decision-making around project design and investment prioritization to support developing member countries in devising stakeholder-informed, climate-resilient integrated urban plans. Accordingly, SPADE was piloted in Hue, Vinh Yen, and Ha Giang in Viet Nam (related to the SGCDP), as well as in Bagerhat and Patuakhali in Bangladesh.

Linking up disaster risk reduction efforts with disaster risk financing, UCCRTF support has also been directed at developing a disaster risk insurance model for public assets, piloted in Hue in light of the city's vast cultural assets and their exposure to flooding, tropical cyclone, and landslide risks. As such, the insurance model in combination with the technical assistance, loan project, and capacity development can combine structural and nonstructural measures to strengthen resilience against climate and disaster risks.

Sources: ADB. 2020. Urban Climate Change Resilience Trust Fund. https://www.livablecities.info/urban-resilience-fund.
ADB. 2017. ADB to Support Development of Green, Resilient Urban Infrastructure in Viet Nam's Secondary Cities. https://www.adb.org/news/adb-support-development-green-resilient-urban-infrastructure-viet-nams-secondary-cities.
ADB. 2017. Viet Nam: Secondary Green Cities Development Project. https://www.adb.org/projects/47274-003/main#project-pds.
Bugler, W. 2019. Resilience Planning Can Uncover Investment Opportunities at the City Level. PreventionWeb. 26 March. https://www.preventionweb.net/news/view/64460.

Green, resilience, and SDG bonds by multilateral development banks. Mirroring the mechanisms and instruments previously presented, multilateral development banks have also successfully issued a variety of bonds on their loan portfolios, including, for instance, the World Bank's 10-year Global Sustainable Development Bond that raised €1.5 billion (approximately $1.76 billion), the climate resilience bond by the European Bank for Reconstruction and Development that raised $700 million, and ADB's multiple issuances under its Green Bond Framework (including climate-resilient growth investments).[62] Building up on those efforts, multilateral development banks can pool together resilience-specific investments into bonds for capital market financing at a much larger scale based on their AAA credit rating.

Although international development organizations provide attractive (affordable) financing to developing countries that further disaster risk reduction measures, it needs to be recognized that the scale of their funding in this area will only supply a fraction of the overall investment needs—other significant public and private sources will have to be mobilized alongside.

[62] World Bank. 2019. World Bank Announces Euro 1.5 Billion 10-Year Sustainable Development Bond in Ireland. Press Release: 16 May. https://www. worldbank.org/en/news/press-release/2019/05/16/world-bank-announces-euro-15-billion-10-year-sustainable-development-bond-in-ireland; EBRD. 2019. World's First Dedicated Climate Resilience Bond, for US$ 700m, Is Issued by EBRD. News: 20 September. https://www.ebrd.com/ news/2019/worlds-first-dedicated-climate-resilience-bond-for-us-700m-is-issued-by-ebrd-.html; ADB. 2020. ADB Green Bonds. https:// www.adb.org/site/investors/adb-green-bonds.

5 Steps toward Enhanced Disaster Risk Reduction Finance

Five steps are recommended for consideration by governments to advance financing of disaster risk reduction.

1. **Getting the basics right**. Regardless of the financing instruments used—from traditional inter-governmental transfers to green bonds and blended finance—it is imperative that government bodies continue their efforts to strengthen fiscal management and good governance. This can ensure both the efficacy and continuity of critical disaster risk reduction efforts and the maximization of related investments. Transparency, accountability, rule of law, and the enforcement of standards and regulations remain the basis on which sustainable finance can build.

2. **Strengthening climate and disaster resilience is a cross-sector endeavor**. Governments need to mainstream these topics across policies and departments, allocate dedicated budgets that are legally safeguarded from politically fluctuating support, require thorough resilience-proofing of any investments, and proactively engage and empower subnational entities through effective vertical coordination of disaster risk management (footnote 17).

3. **What gets measured gets managed**. Based on improved data collection and climate and disaster risk assessments, governments can benefit from a clearer understanding of their risk exposure and related funding needs into resilience infrastructure and nonstructural measures. These can then inform their strategies and plans—including programming with international development organizations—and allow for clearer signaling to the private sector where accelerated investments will be made (footnote 15).

4. **Financing instruments for disaster resilience benefit from standardized terminology and metrics**. Furthermore, innovative financing models require adjustments to national regulations to allow new partnerships and mechanisms. As such, governments should continue to collaborate with the finance industry and international finance institutions to develop and refine assessment, quantification, pricing, and monitoring approaches and methodologies to make resilience projects and vehicles into bankable investments with economic, environmental, and social co-benefits (footnote 27).

5. **Collaborate with partners to devise localized technical solutions for reducing disaster risks**. Multilateral development banks and UN agencies can provide grants and concessional loans—as well as their technical expertise and convening power—to assist in developing and financing location-specific resilience measures. If those are proven effective, they can be scaled-up with the support of global funds and blended finance facilities (footnote 7). Developing countries should also realize the role of multilateral development banks as finance intermediaries for enhanced private sector activity in disaster risk reduction (footnote 5). Moreover, there is an abundance of training courses and tools available to upskill government staff to become familiar with key concepts and more attuned to interacting with private sector actors in devising cofinanced resilience investments.

APPENDIX 1
International Agendas Guiding Disaster Risk Reduction

Sendai Framework for Disaster Risk Reduction (2015)

The Sendai Framework for Disaster Risk Reduction, adopted by the United Nations General Assembly in 2015, is a nonbinding 15-year agreement that recognizes that the State has the primary role to reduce disaster risk, but that responsibility should be shared with other stakeholders including local government, the private sector, and other stakeholders. The Sendai Framework's goal is to substantially reduce disaster risk and losses, including reducing mortality, morbidity, and economic risk and impacts associated with disasters. To this end, it seeks to increase the number of local and national disaster risk strategies.

Source: United Nations. 2015. *Sendai Framework for Disaster Risk Reduction 2015–2030*. New York.

2030 Agenda for Sustainable Development & the United Nations Sustainable Development Goals (2015)

Embedded in the 2030 Agenda, the United Nations Sustainable Development Goals (SDGs) recognize the need to reduce disaster risk by directly referencing the Sendai Framework and developing new goals and targets that will support disaster risk reduction. Indeed, SDG 1 relates to poverty reduction, which will reduce vulnerability to disaster and improve adaptive capacity. SDG 2 aims to ensure sustainable food production and implement resilient agricultural systems. SDG 3 aims to improve well-being at all ages, in part by improving global health early warning and risk reduction systems. SDG 8 strives to promote economic well-being, with the expansion of access to banking and financial services as a priority. SDG 9 states the need for developing resilient infrastructure and SDG 11 explicitly identifies strengthening urban resilience as an aim. SDG 13 focuses solely on climate change action, including awareness raising, early warning, and increasing resilience and adaptive capacity. Finally, SDG 15 aims to improve and conserve terrestrial ecosystems, including by mobilizing sustainable finance mechanism to provide incentives to this end.

Source: United Nations. 2015. *Transforming Our World: The 2030 Agenda for Sustainable Development*. New York.

Paris Agreement under the United Nations Framework Convention on Climate Change (effective 2016)

An agreement within the United Nations Framework Convention on Climate Change (UNFCCC), the Paris Agreement sets out a framework to keep global temperature rise below 2°C compared to pre-industrial baseline and pursue efforts toward 1.5°C to reduce the impacts of climate change. The Paris Agreement is harmonized with the Sendai Framework because it addresses climate-related disaster risk, with the aim of improving adaptive capacity and reducing the risks of and vulnerability to climate change. Presently, there are 195 signatory countries and 187 parties to the Agreement.

Source: United Nations. 2015. *Paris Agreement*. New York.

New Urban Agenda (2016)

The New Urban Agenda, adopted at United Nations Conference on Housing and Sustainable Urban Development (Habitat III) in 2016, relates the principles of the Sendai Framework to the urban context. It outlines the need for cities to sustainably manage their resources and proactively address disaster risk reduction, including through developing and integrating disaster risk reduction strategies into urban development plans, with the overall vision of enabling just, safe, healthy, accessible, affordable, resilient, and sustainable urban settlements that foster prosperity and quality of life for all.

Source: United Nations. 2017. *New Urban Agenda*. New York.

Addis Ababa Action Agenda (2015)

The Addis Ababa Action Agenda (AAAA) was developed at the United Nation's Third International Conference on Financing for Development. The AAAA establishes a framework for financing sustainable development, which will support countries to integrate the goals of the Sendai Framework and achieve the SDGs. The AAAA specifically considers disaster risk reduction, including climate change adaptation, and aims to promote innovative financing mechanisms to support local and national capacity to integrate risk reduction strategies and investments into their development agendas.

Source: United Nations. 2015. *Addis Ababa Action Agenda of the Third International Conference on Financing for Development*. New York.

ASEAN Agreement on Disaster Management and Emergency Response (2005)

The Association of Southeast Asian Nations (ASEAN) Agreement on Disaster Management and Emergency Response (AADMER) is a legally binding regional treaty that lays out disaster risk reduction and management policy within ASEAN. It recognizes the compounding and diffuse nature of disaster risk and, as a result, the need for intraregional cooperation and response. All 10 ASEAN member countries are part of this agreement. The ASEAN Coordinating Centre for Humanitarian Assistance on Disaster Management was established following this agreement.

Source: ASEAN. 2012. ASEAN Agreement on Disaster Management and Emergency Response. Vientiane, 26 July 2005. Vientiane.

Warsaw International Mechanism for Loss and Damage associated with Climate Change Impacts (2013)

Established at the 2013 Conference of the Parties (COP), the Warsaw International Mechanism for Loss and Damage associated with Climate Change Impacts (WIM) aims to mobilize expertise, finance, and improve capacity around loss and damage associated with climate change, including both acute and slow onset events.

Source: UNFCCC. 2013. Warsaw International Mechanism for Loss and Damage associated with Climate Change Impacts (WIM). https://unfccc.int/topics/adaptation-and-resilience/workstreams/loss-and-damage-ld/warsaw-international-mechanism-for-loss-and-damage-associated-with-climate-change-impacts-wim.

APPENDIX 2
Entry Points for Strengthening Disaster Risk Reduction and Its Financing

The Global Assessment Report by the United Nations Office for Disaster Risk Reduction (UNDRR) provides guidance on how to advance resilience against disaster risks along five entry points (Figure A2), as exemplified by the case study of the Hiroshima City Water Bureau (Box A2).[1]

Figure A2: Entry Points for Strengthening Disaster Risk Reduction and Its Financing

Policy and Law

Knowledge

Organization

Finance

Stakeholders

Source: Author.

Policy and law. Disaster risk reduction requires a guiding legislative and regulatory framework to inform development planning, budgeting, as well as programming. It also provides rules and signals to the private sector to comply with and ideally go beyond minimum requirements in future-proofing assets and investments. Policies should also incorporate or at least be aligned with existing regulations and plans around climate change and environmental sustainability.

Organization. Addressing shortfalls in the capacity of the public and private sector actors, making available training programs and tools (also in schools) can help to strengthen human resources, planning, and management skills across government levels and industries to help scaling-up necessary disaster risk reduction measures. Clarifying roles and responsibilities can also help to improve horizontal and vertical coordination in government and open up space for subnational actors to innovate and advance disaster risk reduction initiatives informed by local knowledge and solutions.

Stakeholders. To develop a better database and collate good practices, the engagement of the public sector with actors from the private sector and civil society has to be strengthened—from the national level down to a neighborhood scale and firm level. Furthermore, there is a need to broaden the perspective of disaster risks to

---

[1]   UNDRR. 2019. *Global Assessment Report on Disaster Risk Reduction*. Geneva.

identify different vulnerabilities, for instance, for single-parent households, women, persons with disabilities, children, elderly, or migrants who currently do not have an equal voice in informing government policy.

Knowledge. Improved understanding of climate and disaster risks is an important basis on which actors can be capacitated to take risk-informed decisions. The provision of accurate and freely accessible data together with user-oriented communication and awareness raising can change how risks are perceived and how disaster risk reduction is given importance by different stakeholders. A common platform for knowledge exchange on disaster risk reduction and financing mechanisms is beneficial within countries as well as on a regional level.

Finance. Besides instruments and mechanisms for disaster risk reduction, it is crucial to calculate risk exposure, potential losses and costs, and related investment needs to inform budgeting, cost sharing, and fund design. Tracking disaster risk reduction-related expenditures and investments across departments and government levels can help to identify gaps and improve fiscal transparency and accountability for an otherwise complex topic. Finance for disaster risk reduction also has to be thought-out more widely, taking into account indirect financial implications from nonfinancial incentives, standards, and regulations (e.g., with regard to building codes and development rights).

Box A2: Enhancing Water Supply Continuity in Hiroshima, Japan

The Hiroshima City Water Bureau (HCWB) is responsible for supplying water to Hiroshima City and two neighboring towns (Fuchu and Saka). This region of Japan is particularly susceptible to intense rains and landslides, due to frequent rainfall and the prefecture's location being on alluvial plains surrounded by mountains. HCWB and Hiroshima City have implemented various countermeasures in cooperation with relevant city bureaus (e.g., the fire department) and other utilities to ensure a collaborative response is mobilized when reacting to disasters. As a result of previous heavy rainfall events, Hiroshima City formulated a "Reconstruction Vision upon the Heavy Rainfall Disaster on August 2014" to develop more robust city infrastructure. The HWCB set up a designated team—the Planning and General Affairs Division—within their organizational structure who are mainly responsible for the disaster risk management and emergency response for water within the city. The Civil Engineering Bureau of the Hiroshima Municipal Prefectural Government continues to undertake site inspections assessing the location of each primary water facility using a method specified in Japan's Sediment Disaster Prevention Act. These assessments categorize the risk posed to each site by landslides; as well as quantify the potential risks to infrastructure and threat to human life. To implement the Primary Pipeline Development Plan, the HCWB invested in interconnecting the primary water distribution pipelines around the city to minimize the disruption to the network in the event of a landslide.

Source: World Bank. 2018. *Resilient Water Supply and Sanitation Services. The Case of Japan*. Washington, DC.

APPENDIX 3
Assessment Criteria for Disaster Risk Reduction Finance Instruments

Figure A3 provides a classification of nine criteria that can be used in the identification, evaluation, and decision for or against a particular finance instrument for disaster risk reduction.[2]

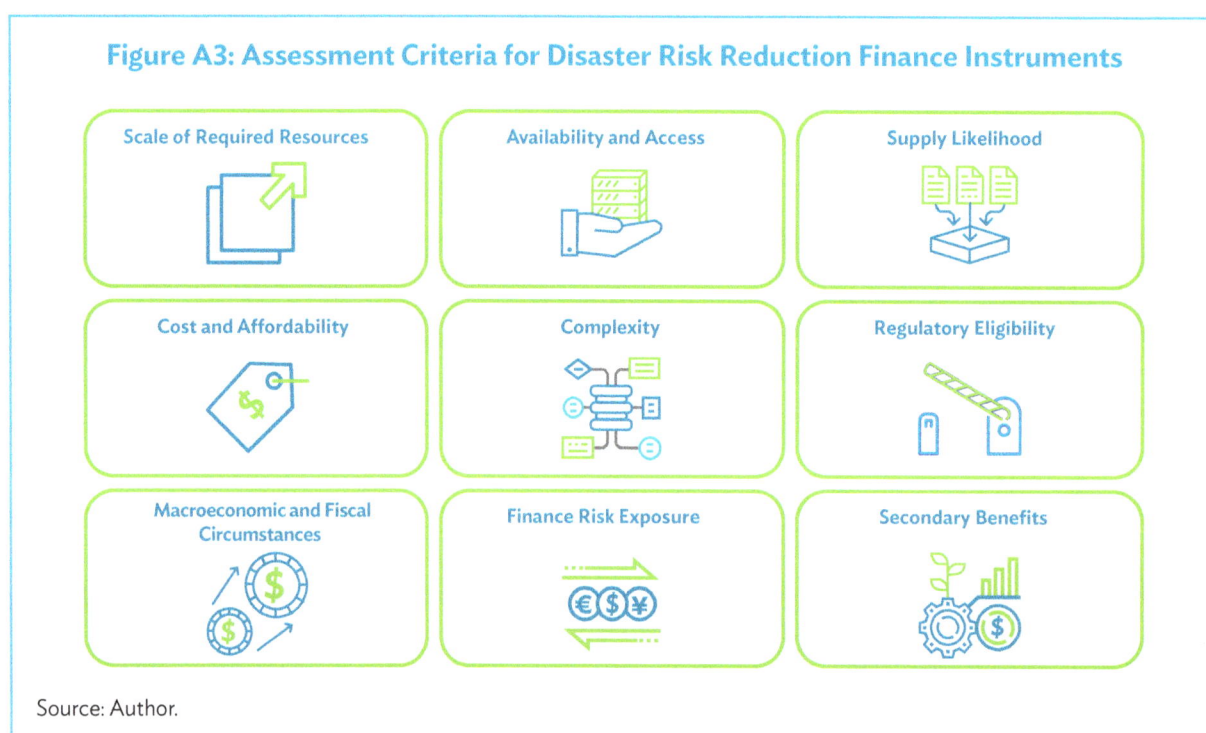

Figure A3: Assessment Criteria for Disaster Risk Reduction Finance Instruments

Source: Author.

Scale of resources. One criterion concerns the scale of resources that an instrument provides versus the scale of resources that an instrument requires. This aspect looks at the financial amount to which an instrument provides access to, e.g., in the international capital market, versus the financial amount that the instrument users would have to provide through their own resources or third-party sources, e.g., required matched funding in a grant scheme.

Availability and access. Another aspect is the availability of and access to an instrument. This relates to a potential instrument user's authority to be eligible to use a certain instrument or the instrument's (dis)allowed

---

2   ADB. 2019. *The Enabling Environment for Disaster Risk Financing in Fiji. Country Diagnostics Assessment.* Manila; UNESCAP. 2019. *The Future of Asian and Pacific Cities. Transformative Pathways Towards Sustainable Urban Development.* Bangkok; World Bank. 2016. *Disaster Risk Finance as a Tool for Development. A Summary of Findings from the Disaster Risk Finance Impact Analytics Project.* Washington, DC.

access to a particular country, e.g., certain countries limit market entry for international reinsurers, which correspondingly make their instruments unavailable to potential domestic users. It also concerns the potential unavailability of an existing instrument for use in a new sector, or the instrument provider may have committed their complete available resource envelope for this instrument already.

Supply likelihood. A third aspect concerns the supply likelihood of an instrument. Under the assumption that resource requirements are met and a potential user is eligible to access a particular instrument, it needs to be checked if the instrument supplier would find a project, product, or program attractive enough to offer their instrument and related finance to the potential recipient. This is best exemplified with an early-stage disaster risk reduction technology that could be financed by green finance focused investors, but may not attract their investment due to a lack of scalability or proven performance.

Cost and affordability. The fourth criterion for assessing the suitability of a finance instrument for disaster risk reduction looks at the cost of the instrument. While there is no lack of various financing products and mechanisms, they will come with different risk pricing and, as such, be more or less affordable to a potential user of an instrument who may instead opt for other finance instruments or sources.

Complexity. Turning to technical capacities, the fifth criterion looks at the complexity of a given instrument. Initial assessments of disaster risk reduction measures remain an obstacle in matching finance supply and demand. In a similar vein, some finance instruments come with a design and mechanisms that may be too difficult for an unexperienced user to understand and properly deploy. While a provider of such instrument may not necessarily be concerned with the complexity of their instrument for the user, it underscores the importance of demand-side actors to seek professional third-party advisory services to critically assess if an instrument fits their skills, experience, financial resources, and risk appetite.

Regulatory eligibility. Linking it back to the institutional elements hindering disaster risk reduction finance, another aspect concerns the regulatory eligibility of an instrument. Depending on a country's legal and regulatory framework, certain instruments may only be offered to particular entities. There may also be certain minimum capitalization requirements, credit ratings, or project sizes that would make an instrument eligible for use or not.

Macroeconomic and fiscal considerations. With particular reference to governments, macroeconomic and fiscal considerations inform in how far an instrument for financing disaster risk reduction may be suitable at a certain time. This aspect, thus, puts an instrument in its broader context as it relates to other monetary activities and, most importantly, commitments. For instance, a low interest rate may make debt instruments very attractive for use; however, if an entity faces already high debt burdens, it may risk a downgrading of its credit rating.

Finance risk exposure. The criterion of finance risk exposure points toward the characteristics of an instrument that may make its user susceptible to certain risks. For example, an instrument offered in a currency different than the user's country currency, the finance would come with foreign exchange fluctuation risks.

Secondary benefits. Lastly, not only considering the financial cost of an instrument, it is worthwhile to assess an instrument's potential secondary benefits. Those could be linked to ease of deploying the instrument in a sector where it has been already tested before. It could also concern the speed with which an instrument could be identified, contractually secured, and deployed. It may also be an instrument that fits a certain institutional structure for use by subnational agencies. Or an instrument may come with capacity development benefits to its suppliers and users, which may open up opportunities to additional instruments in the future.

APPENDIX 4
Disaster Risk Reduction Finance in Mexico and Costa Rica

Mexico's Natural Disaster Prevention Fund (FOPREDEN)

Established following the 1985 Mexico City Earthquake, the National Civil Protection System (SINAPROC) plays a large role in disaster risk reduction in the country. Financed directly by the Ministry of Interior, SINAPROC aims to drive investment into disaster recovery through the Fund for Natural Disasters (FONDEN). FONDEN has a specific fund dedicated to disaster prevention—the Natural Disaster Prevention Fund (FOPREDEN), which focuses exclusively on disaster prevention. FONDEN receives, at a minimum, 0.4% of programmable federal spending under Mexico's Fiscal Responsibility Law (LFPRH), of which an annually determined amount is distributed to FOPREDEN. FOPREDEN funds research, develop, and invest in new technologies, from hard infrastructure like early warning systems to soft interventions like transforming institutional arrangements to better integrate disaster risk reduction into planning and policies. However, the proportion of the FORPREDEN's budget is negligible compared to the Fund for Natural Disasters (FONDEN), which provides funding for post-disaster recovery, underscoring the continued underemphasis on the benefits of ex ante disaster risk reduction financing.

Sources:Kellet, J., A. Caravani, and F. Pichon. 2014. *Financing Disaster Risk Reduction: Towards a Coherent and Comprehensive Approach*. London: ODI.
Marsh & McLennan. 2018. *Climate Resilience 2018 Handbook*. Singapore.
OECD & World Bank. 2019. *Fiscal Resilience to Natural Disaster: Lessons from Country Experiences*. Paris.
UNDP. 2014. Mexico: Country Case Study Report – How Law and Regulation Support Disaster Risk Reduction. New York.

Costa Rica's Approach to Disaster Risk Management and Finance

Susceptible to multiple hazards, Costa Rica boasts a comprehensive legal framework for disaster risk management, embodied by the 2006 formation of the National Risk Management. System (SNPRAE). These legal mechanisms have shifted Costa Rica's focus increasingly toward disaster prevention in recent years, with one subsystem of the Commission specifically dedicated to disaster prevention and mitigation. Indeed, SNPRAE requires that existing disaster risk is incorporated into all state and local budgets and programs. The SNPRAE has mixed-model financing, combining stand-alone financing with sector ministries contributing 3% of their annual surplus to the Fund. However, SNPRAE does not require a dedicated percentage of budget allocated to "disaster" prevention. Funding tends to fluctuate largely due to the Fund's reliance on post-disaster finance. And while there are clearly established roles and responsibilities outlined in legislation, in practice, these roles are held by noncentral government actors and—on a municipal level—the Management Committees tasked with coordinated local disaster risk management often lack the skills or capacity to adequately manage these risks.

Source: Kellet, J., A. Caravani, and F. Pichon. 2014. *Financing Disaster Risk Reduction: Towards a Coherent and Comprehensive Approach*. London: ODI.

APPENDIX 5
Land Value Capture Instruments Applied to Disaster Risk Reduction Finance

One own-source revenue to highlight is land value capture.[3] The advantages of land value capture mechanisms are that they share the cost of infrastructure among beneficiaries, allow greater spatial development control by (subnational) governments, increase their fiscal independence, provide for a faster recovery of externality values created by public investments, and link more strongly revenue generation and local service provision.[4] It provides six mechanisms for governments to finance disaster risk reduction alongside the land development:

(i)   The **sale or lease of public land** can provide cash resources to government, while the sale or lease itself can also be linked to specific development standards around climate and disaster resilience.

(ii) Similarly, **development charges** to investors obtaining land development rights can be used for the provision of infrastructure that reduces disaster risks in the development area.

(iii) The **sale of development rights or density credits** can fulfill the double function of additional funding to disaster risk reduction investments, while also steering higher-density development to lower-risk areas, while making high-risk areas more expensive to develop.

(iv) Applying **land pooling or readjustment** requires a well-established legal framework, under which land owners agree to the partial contribution of their land to redevelopment and sale in exchange for a usually smaller, yet developed and presumably higher-value plot of land within the neighborhood. This, in turn, can allow the government to incorporate resilience into the redeveloped land, at least partially financed through the land sale.

(v)   **Betterment levies** are tax increments on top of existing taxes to represent and refinance for instance disaster risk reduction investments in local infrastructure that increase the resilience of properties against specific disaster events, such as flooding.

(vi) **Tax increment financing**, on the other hand, estimates the expected increase in future property (or other) tax revenue and leverages the difference (increment) between current and future revenues through a bond or loan, which provide—under considerations of disaster risk reduction—the finance for risk mitigating investments in a blighted, previously higher-risk area.

While land value capture mechanisms provide useful additional finance alongside more traditional sources, they often require a solid legal and regulatory system, a carefully drafted local development plan, as well as an effective land management and assessment system.[5]

---

[3]   World Bank. 2018. *Land Value Capture. Investment in Infrastructure*. Washington, DC.
[4]   Sharma, M., R. Teipelke, and S. Hui Li. Forthcoming. Financial Sustainability of Cities. In: ADB. *Contemporary Issues for Livable Asian Cities*. Chapter 5A.
[5]   World Bank. 2019. *Capital Mobilization for City Resilience*. Washington, DC.

Public Sector Nonfinancial Instruments for Disaster Risk Reduction

Although they are technically not instruments to finance disaster risk reduction, there is a range of tools that the public sector can use to indirectly advance disaster risk reduction (Figure A6).[6]

Figure A6: Examples of Public Sector Nonfinancial Instruments for Disaster Risk Reduction

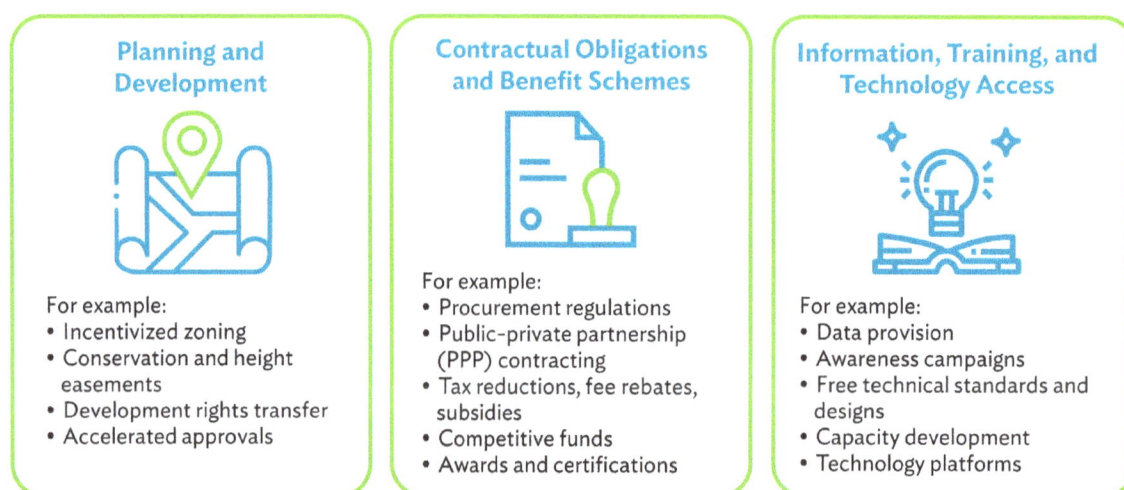

Planning and Development

For example:
- Incentivized zoning
- Conservation and height easements
- Development rights transfer
- Accelerated approvals

Contractual Obligations and Benefit Schemes

For example:
- Procurement regulations
- Public-private partnership (PPP) contracting
- Tax reductions, fee rebates, subsidies
- Competitive funds
- Awards and certifications

Information, Training, and Technology Access

For example:
- Data provision
- Awareness campaigns
- Free technical standards and designs
- Capacity development
- Technology platforms

Source: Author.

Planning and Development

Notwithstanding previously mentioned challenges around rapid spatial development in developing countries, spatial planning and development is a powerful public sector tool in advancing disaster risk reduction. This can be supported by incentivized zoning, conservation and height easements, the transfer of development rights, or resettlement in combination with land provision—all which are steered toward promoting development in areas considered at lower risk to climate and disaster impacts, while development in high-risk zones is restricted. Interlinked with those planning tools is the option of accelerated approvals and service provision in areas where development shall be encouraged, whereby more scrutiny may be given to development applications in disaster-prone areas.

---

[6]   ADB. 2016. Incentives for Reducing Disaster Risk in Urban Areas. Experiences from Da Nang (Viet Nam), Kathmandu Valley (Nepal), and Naga City (Philippines). Manila; Micale, V., B. Tonkonogy, and F. Mazza. 2018. *Understanding and Increasing Finance for Climate Adaptation in Developing Countries.* San Francisco: Climate Policy Initiative & Adelphi.

Contractual Obligations and Benefit Schemes

The public sector is usually the largest client for infrastructure projects. In this role, it is imperative that government authorities carefully adjust procurement regulations and contractual guidelines for public works and related infrastructure projects—including public–private partnerships—to include standards for disaster risk resilience which new assets shall be designed to. Similarly, in the procurement of service contracts, obligations with regard to infrastructure's minimum performance in the event of specific disasters can be defined.[7]

In addition to government investments in trunk infrastructure and public assets, households and firms can play a valuable role in scaling-up disaster risk reduction measures. Therefore, government can provide various incentives, such as value added tax reductions or exemptions on materials for disaster risk reduction projects, property tax reductions for retrofitted properties, license fee rebates for businesses that have put in place business continuity plans, subsidies to companies that are investing in disaster risk reduction technology, and low-cost or free materials and tools for households and micro or small enterprises to upgrade their facilities to increase their resilience against disaster events.[8]

Similar to the abovementioned competitive grants fund, government can provide dedicated funding to private sector and civil society organizations that put forward innovative proposals for local disaster risk reduction efforts. Enterprise development loans by government agencies can also include eligibility criteria with regard to applicants' built-in resilience in their business proposals. Targeting poorer households, existing government safety net programs can incorporate conditionality based on certain disaster risk reduction actions of recipients.[9]

And encouraging local leadership in climate and disaster resilience can also be promoted through awards and certifications, whereby local administrations that advance disaster risk reduction are recognized at the national level, which may provide them access to additional funds and signal to investors that those municipalities are suitable locations for more risk-resilient investments.[10]

Information, Training, and Technology Access

A third area of public sector nonfinancial instruments to advance disaster risk reduction relates to improved understanding and knowledge around climate and disaster resilience. The provision of freely available, accurate, timely, and user-oriented information can help actors to better understand, assess, and act upon risks. Governments can decide to disclose the risk exposure of different land and may mandate private developers to do so equally.[11]

Awareness campaigns around disaster preparedness, emergency response, and, for instance, the usefulness of household and firm disaster insurances can strengthen resilience at both an individual and community level. Making freely available technical standards and designs for resilient infrastructure can help property owners to invest in disaster risk reduction measures, as well as guide local service providers in supporting such retrofits.

[7] OECD. 2018. *Climate-Resilient Infrastructure. Policy Perspectives.* OECD Environment Policy Paper No. 14. Paris.
[8] Benson, C. 2016. *Promoting Sustainable Development through Disaster Risk Management.* ADB Sustainable Development Working Paper Series No. 41. Manila: ADB.
[9] Benson, C. 2016. Promoting Sustainable Development through Disaster Risk Management. ADB Sustainable Development Working Paper Series No. 41. Manila: ADB; Wilkinson, E. et al. 2017. *Delivering Disaster Risk Reduction by 2030. Pathways to Progress.* London: ODI; World Bank. 2015. Fiscal Disaster Risk Assessment: Options for Consideration. Pakistan. Washington, DC.
[10] ADB. 2016. *Incentives for Reducing Disaster Risk in Urban Areas. Experiences from Da Nang (Viet Nam), Kathmandu Valley (Nepal), and Naga City (Philippines).* Manila.
[11] UNDRR. 2019. *Global Assessment Report on Disaster Risk Reduction.* Geneva.

Related to that, training, capacity development, and certification of local firms and craftspeople can have the double benefit of upskilling the local workforce while expanding the supply of suitable service providers.

In a more advanced scenario, governments can also set up a platform of technology providers, facilitate twinning arrangements between utilities or manufacturing firms, and support the transfer of resilient technologies and early-stage financing of local technology developments.[12]

---

[12]   Micale, V., B. Tonkonogy, and F. Mazza. 2018. *Understanding and Increasing Finance for Climate Adaptation in Developing Countries.* San Francisco: Climate Policy Initiative & Adelphi.

Green Bonds in the United States and Europe

Washington, DC's Innovative Financing for Urban Stormwater Management

Under a changing climate, 1-in-100-year storms are expected to become 1-in-25-year events on the Eastern seaboard of the United States (US). In Washington, DC., stormwater runoff from heavy rain events is compounded by the impervious surfaces that comprise 43% of the city's land. To combat this flood risk, Washington, DC. has several innovative finance mechanisms that aim to more effectively manage the urban water cycle, which is imperative considering the impervious surfaces.

One example is the DC Water Environmental Impact Bond (EIB), which was the first EIB established in the US. DC Water and Sewer Authority, with Goldman Sachs and the Calvert Foundation as investors, used this Bond provided funding to manage stormwater runoff and improve local water quality through the construction of green infrastructure. The EIB's funding mechanisms are effectively performance-oriented, where DC Water uses the bond proceeds to fund the construction, with the performance risks shared between DC Water and investors. Payments on the bond are dependent on the "proven success of the environmental intervention as measured by rigorous evaluation"—i.e., outcome payments to investors if runoff reduction is overachieved, no contingent payment for medium achievement, and risk share payment from investors to DC Water if runoff reduction underachieves intended ranges.

Complementing this EIB are the city's stormwater retention credits, which debuted in 2013. These credits are available to most property and/or landowners where land they own could integrate green infrastructure to better retain stormwater. The credits can be sold to developers who would undertake the actual development of this infrastructure or who would need them as part of a trading scheme in other developments where stormwater retention requirements may not be met on-site. Planning and stormwater stipulations mandated in the Clean Water Act drive people to take up the credits, which have also attracted private sector investment in anticipation of increasing trading activity and related profits.

Sources: D.C. Department of Energy and Environment. 2020. Stormwater Retention Credit Trading Program. https://doee.dc.gov/src.
Goldman Sachs. 2016. Fact Sheet: DC Water Environmental Impact Bond. https://www.goldmansachs.com/media-relations/press-releases/current/dc-water-environmental-impact-bond-fact-sheet.pdf.
Poon, L. 2019. D.C.'s 'Historic' Flash Flood May Soon Be Normal. Citylab. 10 July. https://www.bloomberg.com/news/articles/2019-07-10/lessons-from-a-historic-storm-that-flooded-d-c.
Spector, J. 2016. Turning Stormwater Runoff into Everyone's Business. Citylab. 18 March. https://www.bloomberg.com/news/articles/2016-03-18/d-c-s-stormwater-retention-marketplace-turns-runoff-into-everyone-s-business.

NRW.BANK's Green Bond Funds Largest Fluvial Flood Scheme in European Union

A pioneer in the green bond market in Germany, NRW.BANK has invested in green bonds since 2017 and aims to have €300 million (approximately $351 million) invested by 2020. These bonds fund both climate mitigation and adaptation projects as well as clean transportation. Initially, NRW.BANK focused on climate mitigation projects like wind energy and clean transport before expanding into adaptation projects.

Examples of past mitigation projects funded by NRW.BANK's green bonds include e-mobility projects and hydro-fueled public transportation. The bonds also financed a major climate adaptation project—the restoration of the Emscher River and construction of drainage solutions to mitigate riverine flooding. In fact, this was the largest fluvial flood prevention scheme in the European Union, which evidences the crucial role the bond market has to play in financing infrastructure for climate adaptation and disaster risk reduction. Bonds provide additional benefits through pricing advantages and the increasing importance of the environmental, social, and governance (ESG) activities of bond issuers.

Sources: Fatica, S., R. Panzica, and M. Rancan. 2019. *The Pricing of Green Bonds: Are Financial Institutions Special?* JRC Technical Reports – Working Papers in Economics and Finance 2019/7. Luxembourg: European Commission.
NRW.BANK. 2019. Another NRW.BANK Green Bond Placed Successfully. Press Release: 29 January. https://www.nrwbank.com/en/press/pressarchive/2019/190129_PR_Green_Bond.html.
Richter, F. and D. Marques Pereira. 2019. Helping to Build the Green Bond Market. *Environmental Finance*. 22 February. https://www.environmental-finance.com/content/the-green-bond-hub/helping-to-build-the-green-bond-market.html.

APPENDIX 8
Examples of Global Funds Supporting Disaster Risk Reduction

Resilience Finance within the Green Climate Fund

Based in the Republic of Korea, the Green Climate Fund (GCF) was established within the framework of the United Nations Framework Convention on Climate Change (UNFCCC) as a financial mechanism operating entity to assist developing countries in adaptation and mitigation practices to counter climate change. The Fund has eight impact areas, four of which focus on climate resilient sustainable development under

(i)   enhanced livelihoods of the most vulnerable people, communities, and regions;

(ii)   increased health and well-being, and food and water security;

(iii) resilient infrastructure and built environment to climate change threats; and

(iv)   resilient ecosystems.

The other four areas focus on shifting to low-emission sustainable development setting a 50:50 split between adaptation and mitigation.

The Fund uses a range of financial instruments to provide funding which include grants, concessional debt financing, equity, and guarantees. To access funding, institutions are required to go through a rigorous accreditation process where they must demonstrate strong financial, social, environmental, and gender management policies. Accredited entities develop funding proposals, in close consultation with National Designated Authorities (NDAs) or focal points, based on the differing climate finance needs of individual developing countries. Each project approved by the GCF Board must be endorsed by the NDA or focal point.

Additionally, the GCF Readiness Programme provides vulnerable countries with a one-time grant allocation up to $3 million for the formulation of National Adaptation Plans. The GCF has approved $116 million over 48 proposals and 10 country technical assistances to support the preparation of adaptation planning proposals.

Source: Green Climate Fund. 2020. GCF 101: Project Funding. https://www.greenclimate.fund/gcf101/funding-projects/project-funding.

Adaptation Fund

The Adaptation Fund was established under the Kyoto Protocol of the UNFCCC in 2010 and finances concrete adaptation projects and programs in developing nations that are vulnerable to the increasing adverse effects of climate change. Its primary funding comes from a 2% share of proceeds from the Certified Emission Reductions issued by the Kyoto Protocol Clean Development Mechanism. Total commitments of the Fund have reached $765 million.

The Adaptation Fund provides funding to projects or programs of accredited national and multilateral implementing entities. The projects must be endorsed by the target country and align with its national priorities for sustainable development. Other eligibility requirements exist, such as the need for public participation to be included in project design and implementation. Once accredited, projects are submitted for consideration by the Adaptation Fund Board.

Sources:Adaptation Fund. 2020. About the Adaptation Fund. https://www.adaptation-fund.org/about/.
World Bank. 2020. Financial Intermediary Funds (FIFs): Adaptation Fund. https://fiftrustee.worldbank.org/en/about/unit/dfi/fiftrustee/fund-detail/adapt.

APPENDIX 9
Overview of Financial Disaster Risk Management Instruments

The following sections provide an overview of some of the core elements of disaster risk financing as it relates to disaster risk management finance more broadly.

Risk layering. Risk layering describes how different disaster risk finance instruments can be most effectively matched to a particular risk profile (Figure A9).[13] This means that the frequency and/or probability of a disaster event and the severity of its impact (losses) are assessed—those events likely to occur more often with only minor impacts (e.g., localized landslides as part of the annual raining season) may make use of government reserves or smaller budget reallocation, a sufficient instrument to cover the limited recovery, response, and reconstruction costs.

Figure A9: Risk Layering in Disaster Risk Financing

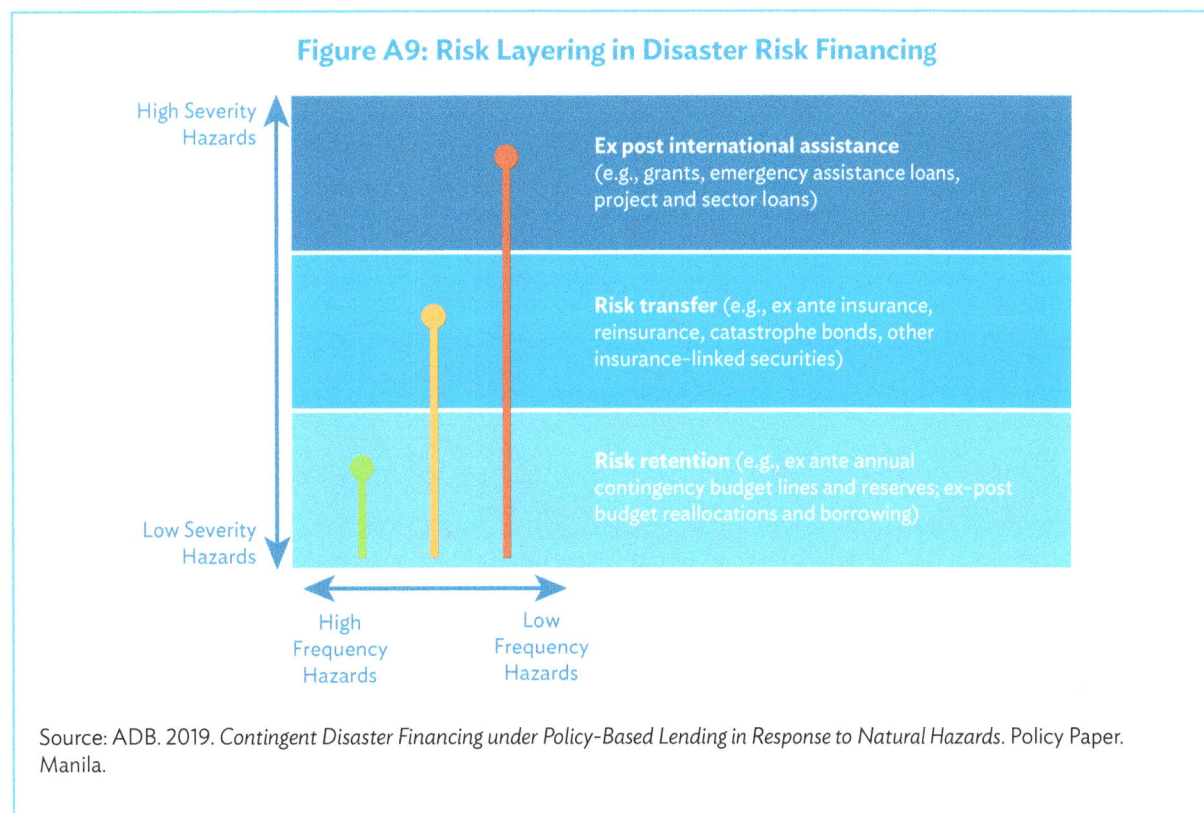

High Severity Hazards

Ex post international assistance (e.g., grants, emergency assistance loans, project and sector loans)

Risk transfer (e.g., ex ante insurance, reinsurance, catastrophe bonds, other insurance-linked securities)

Risk retention (e.g., ex ante annual contingency budget lines and reserves; ex-post budget reallocations and borrowing)

Low Severity Hazards

High Frequency Hazards   Low Frequency Hazards

Source: ADB. 2019. *Contingent Disaster Financing under Policy-Based Lending in Response to Natural Hazards*. Policy Paper. Manila.

---

[13]   ADB. 2019. *The Enabling Environment for Disaster Risk Financing in Fiji. Country Diagnostics Assessment*. Manila.

On the opposite end of the risk spectrum, a rather rare disaster event with major impacts (e.g., an earthquake of magnitude 6 or higher) would not justify the annual large-scale allocation of budgets, but would equally overstrain budget resources and reserves if it were to happen. Therefore, a catastrophic risk transfer (e.g., through a parametric insurance) may be deemed a suitable instrument. Functioning as a scalable concept, risk layering has certain financing instruments where the risk is retained; while other instruments, particularly for high-severity and low-frequency disasters, the risk is transferred. The overall aim is the optimal bundling of such instruments, with the most cost-effective options chosen for each risk layer.

Financial risk management instruments. Financial risk management instruments can play a role in "de-risking" (resilience) investments.[14] They are provided by insurance and financial markets and use both debt and (contingent) equity-related mechanisms. Common examples are: (i) **insurances and risk hedging** (e.g., against disasters triggered by natural hazards and other human-induced risks, political risks such as political violence, expropriation, currency inconvertibility, nonpayment, and contract frustration or currency fluctuations), and (ii) **guarantee instruments** such as performance surety bonds, subordinated debt (e.g., through mezzanine finance), or credit enhancement (e.g., through export credit agencies).

Typically, financial risk management instruments are an essential component of finance, as they lower the risk profile of an investment and thereby reduce the costs of other instruments. This, in turn, can attract investors and/or instrument suppliers who would otherwise be scared off from certain project structures (Box A9.1). Financial risk management instruments can also be complementing risk reduction as a nonstructural measure where the economic cost of investing in structural interventions exceeds their benefits by transferring part of the so-called residual risk.

Box A9.1: Asia-Pacific Climate Finance Fund

The Asia-Pacific Climate Finance Fund (ACLIFF) is an ADB multidonor trust fund established in 2017. The objective of the fund is to support the development and implementation of financial risk management instruments that can help unlock capital for climate investments and improve resilience to the impact of climate change. The aim of the ACLIFF is to i) reduce carbon emissions and increase adaptation measures, ii) leverage climate investment by reducing the risks of adoption and uptake of climate technology in high-priority sectors outlined in nationally-determined contributions and other national climate plans, and iii) offer demand side support for climate risk insurance to address remaining climate risks which could not be efficiently managed by the current adaptation infrastructure.

Source: ADB. 2017. What is the Asia-Pacific Climate Finance Fund? https://www.adb.org/site/funds/funds/asia-pacific-climate-finance-fund.

Disaster risk management instruments. Specifically applied to disaster risks, insurance instruments aim to lower the financial impacts from disaster events and can allow more effective emergency relief, early recovery, and reconstruction financing through the release of assured fast disbursement.[15] Disaster insurance is used by larger entities in the private sector, as well as (sub) sovereigns and state-owned entities in the public sector. In addition, disaster microinsurance plays an important complementing role in allowing households and small firms—particularly at the lower end of economic income—to access post-disaster financing through low-cost asset and livelihood protection.

Specifically looking at Asia and the Pacific, however, nonlife insurance penetration is comparatively low or nearly absent in developing economies, with uninsured disaster losses constituting 95% of losses. International aid

---

[14]   Marsh & McLennan. 2018. *Climate Resilience 2018 Handbook*. Singapore.
[15]   OECD. 2017. *OECD Recommendation on Disaster Risk Financing Strategies*. Paris.

does not significantly address the resulting protection gap in disaster risk financing, as—contrary to common belief—it barely covers 3% of disaster damages.[16] On the flipside, Asia and the Pacific has been the number one target region for international adaptation finance, and risk transfer schemes, and insurance penetration are slowly increasing as well.[17]

Risk transfer has its cost, though, and, following the risk-layered approach outlined above, may not be suitable for all disaster risks.[18] Its price tag should be risk-based and accordingly incentivize risk reduction measures without providing perverse incentives for maladaptation (e.g., for developments in flood-prone areas).[19]

While there are different types for disaster insurances, two have emerged as most suitable: (i) **traditional indemnity-based insurance** where payments are linked to incurred losses; and (ii) **parametric insurance products** where the occurrence of a disaster event is defined by a pre-agreed parameter describing the intensity of the event (e.g., wind speed) as the threshold beyond which an immediate payment will be triggered irrespective of the actual damages incurred (Box A9.2).[20]

Box A9.2: Multi-Actor Coral Reef Insurance in Mexico

Cancun's coastal reef, the region's main tourism attraction, provides one of the most effective natural protective barriers against storms and hurricanes, as they can absorb as much as 97% of wave energy before a wave reaches the shore, dramatically reducing flooding and beach erosion in coastal communities. The health of the coral reef is highly valuable for the region, both in terms of securing assets (such as the many local coastal resorts), as well as generating wealth (coastal tourism, diving). The damage suffered by the reef from human-induced pressures over recent years or during a major hurricane is not only damaging local ecosystems, but also increasing the physical and economic risks to the region.

With support from The Nature Conservancy (TNC), Swiss Re, and the Mexican state, the state government of Quintana Roo established the Coastal Zone Management Trust which links parametric insurance with the protection, conservation, and restoration of the reef. The Trust continuously monitors 60 kilometers of the reef and is prepared to release funds with immediate effect for the restoration of the reef if significant damage is observed. This case serves as an example of the way coral reefs should be valued and protected across the world; and demonstrates how investing in nature can be one of the most effective adaptation measures in the face of increasing climatic events.

Sources: OECD. 2018. *Climate-Resilient Infrastructure. Policy Perspectives.* OECD Environment Policy Paper No. 14. Paris. The Nature Conservancy and Environmental Finance. 2019. *Investing in Nature. Private Finance for Nature-Based Resilience.* London.
Ferrario, F. et al. 2014. The Effectiveness of Coral Reefs for Coastal Hazard Risk Reduction and Adaptation. *Nature Communications.* 5(3794).

---

[16] Suminski, S., A. Panda, and P. J. Lambert. 2019. *Disaster Insurance in Developing Asia: An Analysis of Market-Based Schemes.* ADB Economics Working Paper Series No. 590. Manila: ADB; Benson, C. 2016. *Promoting Sustainable Development through Disaster Risk Management.* ADB Sustainable Development Working Paper Series No. 41. Manila: ADB.

[17] Micale, V., B. Tonkonogy, and F. Mazza. 2018. *Understanding and Increasing Finance for Climate Adaptation in Developing Countries.* San Francisco: Climate Policy Initiative & Adelphi.

[18] Useful "commonly asked questions" and a decision tree for disaster risk financing and insurance can be found in: World Bank. 2014. *Financial Protection against Natural Disasters. From Products to Comprehensive Strategies. An Operational Framework for Disaster Risk Financing and Insurance.* Washington, DC. p. 70–74.

[19] O'Hare, P., I. White, and A. Connelly. 2017. Insuring We Fail? Flood Risk, Vulnerability and the Limits to 'Bouncing Back'. *Town & Country Planning.* April. pp. 160–164.

[20] OECD & ADBI & ADPC. 2018. *Developing the Elements of a Disaster Risk Financing Strategy. Conference Outcomes.* 8–9 May 2018, Bangkok, Thailand. Paris: OECD.

Catastrophe bonds. Catastrophe bonds, developed by the insurance industry to hedge insurers' disaster risk liabilities, make a bridge between bond instruments (discussed in Chapter 4) and risk transfer instruments mentioned above.[21] Catastrophe bonds are linked to the occurrence of a major disaster and are typically issued for a shorter time frame (e.g., 3 years), whereby an insurer issues the bond to the capital market via a special purpose vehicle with the condition that investors would be paid their principal and coupon if no disaster of the defined type and magnitude occurs in a specific location; in the opposite case, investors would lose (parts of) their principal and not be paid a coupon, whereas the insurer would use the principal payment to cover its liability payments to the insured.

Catastrophe bonds are a useful pairing instrument to catastrophe insurance by transferring risk to the capital market—initially used to spread risk by insurance companies, but more recently also adopted by large corporates as well as sovereign governments. They provide additional capitalization which, in turn, allows for a higher leveraging of an entity's resources to cover a larger share of disaster risk.[22] Since catastrophe bonds are focused on disaster events (not) happening, they are primarily a disaster risk transfer instrument, not a disaster risk reduction instrument. However, entities that invest in disaster risk reduction can be recognized for their efforts and obtain more preferential pricing for their catastrophe bonds.

Disaster risk pooling. Combining the aggregation mechanism mentioned in Chapter 4 with risk transfer instruments, (re)insurance for disaster risks provides pooling options.[23] This allows smaller entities (e.g., a pool of municipalities in the Philippines or several Pacific small island developing states) to join an insurance pool, which (i) reduces the uncertainty around disaster risks due to the distributed risk of a disaster occurring and thus triggering insurance pay-outs; (ii) correspondingly lowers the premium payments by pool members; (iii) reduces the operating costs due to joint operation of the insurance pool (including access to much-needed technical capacity); and (iv) allows for profits of the instrument to be retained in the pool, instead of flowing back to the insurance holder, as is typically the case with individual disaster insurance held by a government entity.[24]

Reinsurance. To further mitigate the risk within an insurance instrument, reinsurance can be used to transfer parts of the risk to a third party. This allows for further leveraging of an insurance provider's capital, thereby expanding insurance coverage, and reducing concentrated risk exposure. In the event of a disaster, reinsurance can play a fundamental role in backing up the absorption capacity of insurers for meeting their liabilities to the insured.[25] This is particularly the case when domestic insurers can access global reinsurance services, as the risk is then partly removed outside of the country's financial system.[26] Although still evolving, disaster (re)insurances will become more available, as they allow global providers to diversify their portfolios across different locations where disaster risks are typically uncorrelated. As disaster risk data and modeling further improve, (re)insurance providers will be very interested in expanding their products and services beyond developed economies.[27]

---

[21]   Marsh & McLennan. 2018. *Climate Resilience 2018 Handbook*. Singapore.
[22]   World Bank. 2012. *ASEAN – Advancing Disaster Risk Financing and Insurance in ASEAN Member States: Framework and Options for Implementation*. Volume 1: Main Report. Washington, DC.
[23]   Marsh & McLennan. 2018. *Climate Resilience 2018 Handbook*. Singapore; OECD & ADBI & ADPC. 2018. Developing the Elements of a Disaster Risk Financing Strategy. Conference Outcomes. 8–9 May 2018, Bangkok, Thailand. Paris: OECD; World Bank. 2014. *Financial Protection against Natural Disasters. From Products to Comprehensive Strategies. An Operational Framework for Disaster Risk Financing and Insurance*. Washington, DC.
[24]   For an example of such pool structure, see: ADB. 2018. *Philippine City Disaster Insurance Pool. Rationale and Design*. Manila. p. 30.
[25]   OECD & ADBI & ADPC. 2018. Developing the Elements of a Disaster Risk Financing Strategy. Conference Outcomes. 8–9 May 2018, Bangkok, Thailand. Paris: OECD.
[26]   OECD & ADBI & ADPC. 2018. Developing the Elements of a Disaster Risk Financing Strategy. Conference Outcomes. 8–9 May 2018, Bangkok, Thailand. Paris: OECD.
[27]   World Bank. 2015. *Pacific Catastrophe Risk Insurance Pilot. From Design to Implementation. Some Lessons Learned*. Washington, DC; OECD & ADBI & ADPC. 2018. Developing the Elements of a Disaster Risk Financing Strategy. Conference Outcomes. 8–9 May 2018, Bangkok, Thailand. Paris: OECD.

Glossary

Term	Definition
bond	A bond traditionally takes debt security and sells it to investors serviced by revenue streams from particular projects, general revenue sources and transfers, proceeds or receivables of an infrastructure asset, or revenues from an asset-owning or operating company.
climate change	A change in the state of the climate that can be identified by changes in the mean and/or the variability of its properties and that persists for an extended period, typically decades or longer. Climate change may be due to natural internal processes or external forces, or to persistent anthropogenic changes in the composition of the atmosphere or in land use.
climate change adaptation	The process of adjustment to actual or expected climate and its effects. In human systems—including with regard to infrastructure—adaptation seeks to moderate or avoid harm or exploit beneficial opportunities.
climate co-benefits	The benefits—including social, environmental, and economic—that climate adaptation and disaster risk management investments would yield even in the absence of climate change or disaster risk.
debt-type finance	Debt-type finance is borrowed capital and primarily comes from loans (which can be market-based or concessional and are provided by development partners and commercial lenders) and bonds (which are usually issued by firms or governments and can be traded in the market).
disaster risk	The potential loss of life, injury, or destroyed or damaged assets which could occur to a system, a society, or a community in a specific period of time, determined probabilistically as a function of hazard, exposure, vulnerability, and capacity.
disaster risk management	The application of disaster risk reduction policies and strategies to prevent new disaster risk, reduce existing disaster risk, and manage residual risk, contributing to the strengthening of resilience and reduction of disaster losses.
disaster risk reduction	Preventing new and reducing existing disaster risk and managing residual risk, all of which contribute to strengthening resilience and, therefore, to the achievement of sustainable development.
equity-type finance	Equity-type finance are listed (in the stock exchange) or unlisted (privately held) ownership shares in an investment, whereby the '"profit" does not come from usually fixed and regular interest payments as in the case of most debt-type finance, but from variable and less regular dividends. Due to the higher risk profile of equity-type finance in contrast to debt-type finance, equity-type finance bears the chance of higher returns as well as losses.
grant-type finance	Grant-type finance is usually provided by upper-level governments or international development partners through earmarked grants (for particular purposes) and unconditional (non-earmarked) grants, with other types of transfers and subsidies forming part of direct and indirect non-repayable finance.

continued on next page

Glossary *continued*

Term	Definition
own-source revenues	Own-source revenues are the resources that an entity—for instance, a provincial government—can generate through its own processes, typically from taxes and non-tax sources, such as tariffs, fees, charges, fines, sales, and leases.
resilience	The ability of a system, community, or society exposed to hazards to resist, absorb, accommodate, adapt to, transform, and recover from the effects of a hazard in a timely and efficient manner, including through the preservation and restoration of its essential basic structures and functions through risk management.

Sources: GFDRR. 2015. Unlocking the 'Triple Dividend' of Resilience. Washington, DC. IPCC. 2018. Annex I: Glossary [Matthews, J. B. R. (ed.)]. In: Masson-Delmotte, V. et al. (eds.). Global Warming of 1.5°C. An IPCC Special Report on the impacts of global warming of 1.5°C above pre-industrial levels and related global greenhouse gas emission pathways, in the context of strengthening the global response to the threat of climate change, sustainable development, and efforts to eradicate poverty. Geneva. UNDRR Terminology on Disaster Risk Reduction. http://www.preventionweb.net/english/professional/terminology/.

References

Adaptation Fund. 2020. About the Adaptation Fund. https://www.adaptation-fund.org/about/.

African Development Bank. 2018. African Development Bank Rolls Out Programme to Boost climate Risk Financing and Insurance for African Countries. News: 29 October. https://www.afdb.org/en/news-and-events/african-development-bank-rolls-out-programme-to-boost-climate-risk-financing-and-insurance-for-african-countries-18618.

ADB. 2011. Asia 2050: *Realizing the Asian Century*.

ADB. 2013. *Investing in Resilience. Ensuring a Disaster-Resistant Future*. Manila.

ADB. 2015. *Strengthening City Disaster Risk Financing in Viet Nam*. Manila.

ADB. 2016. *Incentives for Reducing Disaster Risk in Urban Areas. Experiences from Da Nang (Viet Nam), Kathmandu Valley (Nepal), and Naga City (Philippines)*. Manila.

ADB. 2016. *Report and Recommendation of the President to the Board of Directors. Proposed Policy-Based Loan. Cook Islands: Disaster Resilience Program (50212-001)*. Manila.

ADB. 2017. *Catalyzing Green Finance. A Concept for Leveraging Blended Finance for Green Development*. Manila.

ADB. 2017. *Disaster Risk Assessment for Project Preparation. A Practical Guide*. Manila.

ADB. 2017. *Disaster Risk Management and Country Partnership Strategies. A Practical Guide*. Manila.

ADB. 2017. *Integrated Disaster Risk Management Fund – Annual Report*. Manila.

ADB. 2017. *Meeting Asia's Infrastructure Needs*. Manila.

ADB. 2018. ADB to Climate-Proof Nuku'alofa Electricity Network in Tonga. News Release: 18 June. Manila.

ADB. 2018. *Philippine City Disaster Insurance Pool. Rationale and Design*. Manila.

ADB. 2019. *ADF 13 Thematic Pool*. Manila.

ADB. 2019. *Contingent Disaster Financing under Policy-Based Lending in Response to Natural Hazards. Policy Paper*. Manila.

ADB. 2019. *Report and Recommendation of the President to the Board of Directors. Proposed Loan People's Republic of China: Shandong Green Development Fund Project (51194-001)*. Manila.

ADB. 2019. *Strategy 2030 Operational Plan for Priority 3: Tackling Climate Change, Building Climate and Disaster Resilience, and Enhancing Environmental Sustainability, 2019–2024*. Manila.

ADB. 2019. Supporting Disaster Risk Management: Disaster Risk Reduction Financing Mechanism and Disaster Response Facility. Asian Development Fund (ADF) ADF 12 Midterm Review Meeting: 27–28 February, Manila, Philippines. Manila.

ADB. 2019. *The Enabling Environment for Disaster Risk Financing in Fiji. Country Diagnostics Assessment*. Manila.

ADB. 2020. *ADB Green Bonds*. https://www.adb.org/site/investors/adb-green-bonds.

ADB. 2020. Infographic: The benefits of the Spatial Data Analysis Explorer to project officers. https://www.livablecities.info/spatial-data-analysis-explorer.

ADB. 2020. Urban Climate Change Resilience Trust Fund. https://www.adb.org/site/funds/funds/urban-climate-change-resilience-trust-fund.

ADB. 2020. Urban Climate Change Resilience Trust Fund. https://www.livablecities.info/urban-resilience-fund.

ASEAN. 2012. ASEAN Agreement on Disaster Management and Emergency Response. Vientiane, 26 July 2005. Vientiane.

Benson, C. 2016. *Promoting Sustainable Development through Disaster Risk Management*. ADB Sustainable Development Working Paper Series No. 41. Manila: ADB.

C40 Cities Finance Facility. 2017. *Explainer: How to Finance Urban Infrastructure. London*: C40/GIZ.

Caldecott, B. 2018. *Stranded Assets and the Environment*. Abingdon: Routledge.

Chan, C. and N. Amerasinghe. 2018. *Deploying Adaptation Finance for Maximum Impact*. Commentary. Washington DC: World Resources Institute.

Climate Bonds Initiative. 2018. *Green Securitisation. Unlocking Finance for Small-Scale Low Carbon Projects*. Briefing Paper: March. London.

Climate Bonds Initiative. 2019. *Climate Resilience Principles. A Framework for Assessing Climate Resilience Investments*. London.

COP23. 2017. Fiji's Green Bond. https://cop23.com.fj/fiji-green-bond/#:~:text=In%20October%202017%2C%20Fiji%20became,climate%20change%20mitigation%20and%20adaption.

Crick, F. et al. 2019. *Delivering Climate Finance at the Local Level to Support Adaptation: Experiences of County Climate Funds in Kenya*. Nairobi: ADA Consortium.

D.C. Department of Energy and Environment. 2020. Stormwater Retention Credit Trading Program. https://doee.dc.gov/src.

Department of Home Affairs. 2018. *National Disaster Rik Reduction Framework*. Brisbane.

EBRD. 2019. World's First Dedicated Climate Resilience Bond, for US$700m, Is Issued by EBRD. News: 20 September. https://www.ebrd.com/news/2019/worlds-first-dedicated-climate-resilience-bond-for-us-700m-is-issued-by-ebrd-.html.

EBRD. 2020. EBRD Green Cities. Website. https://www.ebrdgreencities.com/.

European Commission. 2018. *Climate Change Adaptation of Major Infrastructure Projects. A Stock-Taking of Available Resources to Assist the Development of Climate Resilient Infrastructure*. Brussels.

Fatica, S., R. Panzica, and M. Rancan. 2019. The Pricing of Green Bonds: Are Financial Institutions Special? JRC Technical Reports – Working Papers in Economics and Finance 2019/7. Luxembourg: European Commission.

Ferrario, F. et al. 2014. *The Effectiveness of Coral Reefs for Coastal Hazard Risk Reduction and Adaptation.* Nature Communications 5(3794).

GFDRR. 2020. Global Facility for Disaster Reduction and Recovery. https://www.gfdrr.org/en/global-facility-disaster-reduction-and-recovery.

Goldman Sachs. 2016. Fact Sheet: DC Water Environmental Impact Bond. https://www.goldmansachs.com/media-relations/press-releases/current/dc-water-environmental-impact-bond-fact-sheet.pdf.

Green Climate Fund. 2020. GCF 101: Project Funding. https://www.greenclimate.fund/gcf101/funding-projects/project-funding.

IFC. 2017. A Green Bond to Help Fiji Secure a Greener Future. https://www.ifc.org/wps/wcm/connect/news_ext_content/ifc_external_corporate_site/news+and+events/news/cm-stories/fiji-green-bond-for-a-greener-future.

IPCC. 2014. Asia. In: Climate Change 2014: Impacts, Adaptation, and Vulnerability. Part B: Regional Aspects. Contribution of Working Group II to the Fifth Assessment Report of the Intergovernmental Panel on Climate Change. New York.

Jackson, D. 2011. *Effective Financial Mechanisms at the National and Local Level for Disaster Risk Reduction.* Paper Written for the Mid Term Review of the UNISDR Hyogo Framework for Action. New York: United Nations Capital Development Fund.

Jenny, H. et al. 2020. *Catalyzing Climate Finance with the Shandong Green Development Fund.* ADB Briefs: 144. Manila.

Kellet, J., and A. Caravani. 2013. *Financing Disaster Risk Reduction. A 20 Year Story of International Aid.* London: ODI & GFDRR.

Kellet, J., A. Caravani, and F. Pichon. 2014. *Financing Disaster Risk Reduction: Towards a Coherent and Comprehensive Approach.* London: ODI.

Kidney, S. 2017. Deep-Dive: Green Synthetic Securitisation Deal: Frees USD 2bn of Capital for Green Investments - Crédit Agricole and Mariner Investment Group Take the Plunge. Climate Bonds Initiative: 13 March. https://www.climatebonds.net/2017/03/deep-dive-green-synthetic-securitisation-deal-frees-usd-2bn-capital-green-investments-cr%C3%A9dit.

Marsh & McLennan. 2018. *Climate Resilience 2018 Handbook.* Singapore.

Maxwell, D. 2017. *Valuing Natural Capital: Future Proofing Business and Finance.* Abingdon: Routledge.

Micale, V., B. Tonkonogy, and F. Mazza. 2018. *Understanding and Increasing Finance for Climate Adaptation in Developing Countries.* San Francisco: Climate Policy Initiative & Adelphi.

The Nature Conservancy and Environmental Finance. 2019. *Investing in Nature. Private Finance for Nature-Based Resilience.* London.

NRW.BANK. 2019. Another NRW.BANK Green Bond Placed Successfully. Press Release: 29 January. https://www.nrwbank.com/en/press/pressarchive/2019/190129_PR_Green_Bond.html.

NWB Bank. 2019. *SDG Housing Bonds. Sustainable Indicator Report 2019*. The Hague.

ODI & World Bank. 2015. *Unlocking the 'Triple Dividend' of Resilience. Why Investing in Disaster Risk Management Pays Off*. London and Washington, DC.

OECD & ADBI & ADPC. 2018. Developing the Elements of a Disaster Risk Financing Strategy. Conference Outcomes. 8–9 May 2018, Bangkok, Thailand. Paris: OECD.

OECD. 2017. *OECD Recommendation on Disaster Risk Financing Strategies*. Paris.

OECD. 2018. *Climate-Resilient Infrastructure. Policy Perspectives*. OECD Environment Policy Paper No. 14. Paris.

O'Hare, P., I. White, and A. Connelly. 2017. Insuring We Fail? Flood Risk, Vulnerability and the Limits to 'Bouncing Back'. *Town & Country Planning*. April. pp. 160–164.

PBSP Disaster Risk Reduction and Management website. https://www.pbsp.org.ph/?page_id=10495.

PDRF. 2020. Emergency Operation Center. https://www.pdrf.org/eoc/functions/

Poon, L. 2019. D.C.'s 'Historic' Flash Flood May Soon Be Normal. Citylab. 10 July. https://www.bloomberg.com/news/articles/2019-07-10/lessons-from-a-historic-storm-that-flooded-d-c.

Refocus. 2017. *Leveraging Catastrophe Bonds. As a Mechanism for Resilience Infrastructure Project Finance*. http://www.refocuspartners.com/wp-content/uploads/2017/02/RE.bound-Program-Report-December-2015.pdf.

Resch, E. et al. 2018. *Mainstreaming, Accessing and Institutionalising Finance for Climate Change Adaptation. Action on Climate Today Learning Paper*. Oxford: Oxford Policy Management.

Richter, F. and D. Marques Pereira. 2019. Helping to Build the Green Bond Market. *Environmental Finance*. 22 February. https://www.environmental-finance.com/content/the-green-bond-hub/helping-to-build-the-green-bond-market.html.

Sharma, M., R. Teipelke, and S. Hui Li. Forthcoming. Financial Sustainability of Cities. In: ADB. *Contemporary Issues for Livable Asian Cities*. Chapter 5A.

Shee, A., C. G. Turvey, and L. You. 2019. Design and Rating of Risk-Contingent Credit for Balancing Business and Financial Risks for Kenyan Farmers. *Applied Economics* 51(50). pp. 5,447–5,465.

Smith, E. 2020. The numbers suggest the green investing 'mega trend' is here to stay. https://www.cnbc.com/2020/02/14/esg-investing-numbers-suggest-green-investing-mega-trend-is-here.html.

Spector, J. 2016. Turning Stormwater Runoff into Everyone's Business. Citylab. 18 March. https://www.bloomberg.com/news/articles/2016-03-18/d-c-s-stormwater-retention-marketplace-turns-runoff-into-everyone-s-business.

Suminski, S., A. Panda, and P. J. Lambert. 2019. *Disaster Insurance in Developing Asia: An Analysis of Market-Based Schemes*. ADB Economics Working Paper Series No. 590. Manila: ADB.

Swiss Re. 2017. *Barisal: Helping a City Prepare for Climate Change*. Zurich.

Tamil Nadu Urban Infrastructure Financial Services Limited. 2019. Tamil Nadu Urban Development Fund. About Us. http://tnuifsl.com/tnudf.asp.

UNDP. 2014. Mexico: *Country Case Study Report – How Law and Regulation Support Disaster Risk Reduction*. New York.

UNDRR. 2015. *Disaster Risk Reduction Private Sector Partnership.* Geneva.

UNDRR. 2017. *Disaster-Related Data for Sustainable Development – Sendai Framework Data Readiness Review 2017, Global Summary Report.* Geneva.

UNDRR. 2019. *Disaster Risk Reduction in the Philippines. Status Report 2019.* Bangkok.

UNDRR. 2019. *Global Assessment Report on Disaster Risk Reduction.* Geneva.

UNESCAP. 2019. *The Future of Asian and Pacific Cities. Transformative Pathways Towards Sustainable Urban Development.* Bangkok.

UNFCCC. 2013. Warsaw International Mechanism for Loss and Damage Associated with Climate Change Impacts (WIM). https://unfccc.int/topics/adaptation-and-resilience/workstreams/loss-and-damage-ld/warsaw-international-mechanism-for-loss-and-damage-associated-with-climate-change-impacts-wim.

United Nations. 2008. *Private Sector Activities in Disaster Risk Reduction. Good Practices and Lessons Learned.* Bonn.

United Nations. 2015. *Addis Ababa Action Agenda of the Third International Conference on Financing for Development.* New York.

United Nations. 2015. *Paris Agreement.* New York.

United Nations. 2015. *Sendai Framework for Disaster Risk Reduction 2015–2030.* New York.

United Nations. 2015. *Transforming Our World: The 2030 Agenda for Sustainable Development.* New York.

United Nations. 2017. New Urban Agenda. New York.

United Nations. 2019. *United Nations Sustainable Development Cooperation Framework. Internal Guidance.* New York.

UN Inter-Agency Task Force on Financing for Development. 2019. Climate Finance, Disaster Risk and Environmental Resilience. Website. https://developmentfinance.un.org/climate-finance-disaster-risk-and-environmental-resilience.

Vaijhala, S. and J. Rhodes. 2018. *Resilience Bonds: A Business-Model for Resilient Infrastructure.* Field Actions Science Reports Special Issue 18. pp. 58–63.

Villacin, D. T. 2017. *A Review of Philippine Government Disaster Financing for Recovery and Reconstruction.* Discussion Paper Series No. 2017-21. Manila: Philippine Institute for Development Studies.

Wilkinson, E. et al. 2017. *Delivering Disaster Risk Reduction by 2030. Pathways to Progress.* London: ODI.

World Bank. 2012. *ASEAN – Advancing Disaster Risk Financing and Insurance in ASEAN Member States: Framework and Options for Implementation.* Volume 1: Main Report. Washington, DC.

World Bank. 2012. *Disaster Risk Management and Multilateral Development Banks. An Overview.* Washington, DC.

World Bank. 2013. *Financing Post-Disaster Recovery and Reconstruction Operations: Developing an Institutional Mechanism to Ensure the Effective Use of Financial Resources.* Washington, DC.

World Bank. 2014. *Financial Protection against Natural Disasters. From Products to Comprehensive Strategies. An Operational Framework for Disaster Risk Financing and Insurance.* Washington, DC.

World Bank. 2014. *Understanding Risk in an Evolving World. Emerging Best Practices in Natural Disaster Risk Assessment.* Washington, DC.

World Bank. 2014. *World Bank Group Directive: Country Engagement.* Washington, DC.

World Bank. 2015. *Fiscal Disaster Risk Assessment: Options for Consideration. Pakistan.* Washington, DC.

World Bank. 2015. *Pacific Catastrophe Risk Insurance Pilot. From Design to Implementation. Some Lessons Learned.* Washington, DC.

World Bank. 2015. *World Bank Group Development Solutions for Disaster Risk Finance.* Washington, DC.

World Bank. 2016. *Disaster Risk Finance as a Tool for Development. A Summary of Findings from the Disaster Risk Finance Impact Analytics Project.* Washington, DC.

World Bank. 2016. *Towards a Regional Approach to Disaster Risk Finance in Asia.* Discussion Paper. Washington, DC.

World Bank. 2017. *Resilient Infrastructure Public–Private Partnerships (PPPs): Contracts and Procurement. The Case of Japan.* Washington, DC.

World Bank. 2018. *Furthering Disaster Risk Finance in the Pacific. Increasing Financial Protection for Fourteen Pacific Island Countries.* Washington, DC.

World Bank. 2018. *IBRD/IDA/IFC/MIGA Guidance: Country Engagement.* Washington, DC.

World Bank. 2018. *Land Value Capture. Investment in Infrastructure.* Washington, DC.

World Bank. 2018. *Resilient Water Supply and Sanitation Services. The Case of Japan.* Washington, DC.

World Bank. 2019. *Capital Mobilization for City Resilience.* Washington, DC.

World Bank. 2019. *Lifelines: The Resilient Infrastructure Opportunity.* Washington, DC.

World Bank. 2019. World Bank Announces Euro 1.5 Billion 10-year Sustainable Development Bond in Ireland. Press Release: 16 May. https://www.worldbank.org/en/news/press-release/2019/05/16/world-bank-announces-euro-15-billion-10-year-sustainable-development-bond-in-ireland.

World Bank. 2020. Financial Intermediary Funds (FIFs): Adaptation Fund. https://fiftrustee.worldbank.org/en/about/unit/dfi/fiftrustee/fund-detail/adapt.

Wouter Botzen W. J. et al. 2019. Integrated Disaster Risk Management and Adaptation. In: Mechler R. et al., eds. *Loss and Damage from Climate Change. Climate Risk Management, Policy and Governance.* Springer, Cham. https://doi.org/10.1007/978-3-319-72026-5_12.

www.ingramcontent.com/pod-product-compliance
Lightning Source LLC
Chambersburg PA
CBHW041121280326
41928CB00061B/3474